Mezzo-Soprano/Belter Volume 4

The Singer's Musical Theatre Anthology

A collection of songs from the musical stage, categorized by voice type. The selections are presented in their authentic settings, excerpted from the original vocal scores.

Compiled and Edited by Richard Walters

ISBN 1-4234-0024-0

7777 W. Bluemound Rd. P.O. Box 13819 Milwaukee, WI 53213

Visit Hal Leonard Online at
www.halleonard.com

Foreword

When I conceived and compiled the first volumes of *The Singer's Musical Theatre Anthology*, released in 1987, I couldn't have possibly imagined the day when I would be writing the foreword for Volume 4. Such a venture is made possible only by the lively and sustained interest of singing actors of all descriptions, be they students or professionals. As a researcher I can only present you with practical choices from existing theatre literature. Without the dedicated pursuit of that music by people such as you, dear reader, these collections would remain on a shelf, unopened.

Volume 4 allows inclusion of songs from shows opened since Volume 3 (released in 2000), as well as a continuing, deeper look into both classic and contemporary musical theatre repertory. As has been the case with each of the solo voice volumes in this series, songs are chosen with many types of talent in mind. All songs do not suit all singers. It is good and natural for any performer to stretch as far as possible, attempting diverse material. But it is also very important ultimately to know what you do well. That is an individual answer, based on your voice, your temperament and your look. This collection has enough variety of songs that any interested performer should be able to find several viable choices.

You will come up with a more individual interpretation, conjured from the ground up in the manner that all the best actors work, if you learn a song on your own, building it into your unique singing voice, *without* imitating a recorded performance. Particularly try to avoid copying especially famous renditions of a song, because you can probably only suffer in the comparison. Would you learn a role from Shakespeare, Shaw or Edward Albee solely by mimicking a recording, film or video/DVD of it? Your answer had better be *of course not!* The same needs to be true of theatre music. After you know the notes and lyrics very well, study the character's stated and unstated motivations and thoughts to come up with your own performance. Explore your own ideas about musical and vocal phrasing to express the character's emotions. In other words, make a song your own, and no one can take it away from you. It's yours for life.

Original keys are used exclusively in this edition. Sometimes these reflect the composer's musical/vocal concept, and sometimes they are merely the keys best suited to the original performers. Still, they give a singer a very good idea of the desired vocal timbre for a song as presented in its authentic theatre context. There are general vocal guidelines for voice types in theatre music, but these are not in stone. A soprano with a good belt will be able to sing songs from the soprano volumes as well as the mezzo-soprano/belter volumes. Belters may decide to work on their "head voice" in soprano songs. Men who have voices that lie between tenor and baritone, commonly called "baritenors" (a common range in contemporary musical theatre), may find songs in both the tenor and baritone/bass volumes.

In my foreword for Volume 3 of *The Singer's Musical Theatre Anthology*, written in 2000, I stated that the movie musical was dead. What a difference five years makes! The genre appears to be gaining a little steam at this writing, evidence of the continued relevance of musical theatre to a wider audience.

The books comprising Volume 4 of this series would not have been possible without the enthusiastic help of Brian Dean as assistant editor, and I thank him heartily.

All the selections from all volumes of this series, including duets, total nearly 700 songs. A marathon performance of all the songs in all volumes of *The Singer's Musical Theatre Anthology* would take more than 40 hours. What fun that would be!

Richard Walters,
December, 2005

THE SINGER'S MUSICAL THEATRE ANTHOLOGY

Mezzo-Soprano/Belter Volume 4

Contents

ABOUT THE SHOWS

The material in this section is by Stanley Green, Richard Walters, Brian Dean, and Robert Viagas, some of which was previously published elsewhere.

AIDA

MUSIC: Elton John
LYRICS: Tim Rice
BOOK: Linda Woolverton, Robert Falls and David Henry Hwang
DIRECTOR: Robert Falls
CHOREOGRAPHER: Wayne Cilento
OPENED: 3/23/00, New York; a run of 1,852 performances

Aida is based on the story of the 1871 opera by Giuseppe Verdi (libretto by Antonio Ghislanzoni) about an Ethiopian princess (Aida) who is captured during wartime by the enemy Egyptians. Radames, an Egyptian general, and Aida fall in love ("The Past is Another Land"). Aida is scorned by the daughter of the Egyptian King, Amneris, who is also in love with Radames. Much later, Radames plans to call off his wedding to Amneris to be with Aida, but Aida convinces him to keep up appearances so she can flee from captivity with her father. Amneris overhears their exchange, and realizes that their marriage is a sham ("I Know the Truth"). At their parting, Radames and Aida wonder if their love was doomed at the outset. The story ends tragically with the death of the two lovers.

ANNIE GET YOUR GUN

MUSIC AND LYRICS: Irving Berlin
BOOK: Herbert Fields and Dorothy Fields
DIRECTOR: Joshua Logan
CHOREOGRAPHER: Helen Tamiris
OPENED: 5/16/46, New York; a run of 1,147 performances

Irving Berlin's musical biography of scrappy gal sharpshooter Annie Oakley earned standing ovations for Broadway stars of two generations: the original, Ethel Merman, in the 1940s and Bernadette Peters in the 1990s. The tune-packed musical traces Annie's rise from illiterate hillbilly to international marksmanship star as she is discovered and developed in the traveling "Buffalo Bill's Wild West Show." Annie falls hard for the show's chauvinistic male star, Frank Butler, and romance blossoms, right up until she begins to outshine Frank. "I Got Lost in His Arms" sees Annie dreaming of her future with Frank. In the end, after quarrelling, the two fall into each other's arms in marriage. The movie version was originally to have starred Judy Garland, but after she was fired from the set, Betty Hutton played the role opposite Howard Keel in the 1950 release. The major Broadway revival starring Peters opened in 1999; Reba McEntire also enjoyed special acclaim as Annie in that production.

ASPECTS OF LOVE

MUSIC: Andrew Lloyd Webber
LYRICS: Don Black and Charles Hart
BOOK: Andrew Lloyd Webber
DIRECTOR: Trevor Nunn
CHOREOGRAPHER: Gillian Lynne
OPENED: 4/8/90, New York; a run of 377 performances

Aspects of Love is based on an autobiographical novel by David Garnett, a nephew of Virginia Woolf. The show had an intimate production style, with orchestrations that threw out the brass in favor of a chamber music sound. It follows a group of characters over nearly two decades of interweaving relationships. The story begins with a 17-year-old boy, Alex, who is infatuated with an actress, Rose, in her mid-20s. The actress eventually has a love affair with Alex's uncle, and they marry. Along the way almost everyone winds up in love with, or broken-hearted by, all the others. The plot is emotionally complex, as are the characters and their relationships. Rose begs Alex to stay with her in "Anything But Lonely, " but as she left him years before, so too will Alex turn her down.

AVENUE Q

MUSIC AND LYRICS: Robert Lopez and Jeff Marx
BOOK: Jeff Whitty
DIRECTOR: Jason Moore
CHOREOGRAPHER: Ken Roberson
OPENED: 7/31/03, New York; still running as of December 2005

Avenue Q is an ironic homage to *Sesame Street*, though the puppet characters are much more adult, dealing with topics such as loud lovemaking, closeted homosexuality, and internet porn addiction. The puppeteers are onstage, acting and singing for their characters, but there are also humans in the production. The story deals with a young college graduate, Princeton, who learns how to live life and find love in New York. Along the way we meet the many tenants in his apartment building on Avenue Q. Princeton and his love interest Kate Monster hit some rocky times, and as they break up, Kate sadly muses "There's a Fine, Fine Line" between a lover and a friend.

THE BEAUTIFUL GAME

MUSIC: Andrew Lloyd Webber
LYRICS AND BOOK: Ben Elton
DIRECTOR: Robert Carsen
CHOREOGRAPHER: Meryl Tankard
OPENED: 9/26,00, London, closed 9/1/01

The "beautiful game" of the title is football (soccer). ("The Beautiful Game" is a common phrase used to describe soccer in the world outside the U.S.) Lloyd Webber and playwright Ben Elton's original story is a tale of teenagers coming of age in Belfast, Ireland, from 1969-1972, a battleground between warring factions of Catholics and Protestants. The teenagers are caught up in that atmosphere, at first competitively on the football field, but eventually their clashes occur on the street as they transition from sweet youths to angry adults, carried away in Nationalistic fever, capable of murder. Star-crossed lovers, Del, a Protestant, and Christine, a Catholic, eventually escape to New York to have a life together. Christine explains her relationship with Del to one of her Catholic friends in "Our Kind of Love," an anthem of love knowing no boundaries.

BELLS ARE RINGING

MUSIC: Jule Styne
BOOK AND LYRICS: Betty Comden and Adolph Green
DIRECTOR: Jerome Robbins
CHOREOGRAPHERS: Jerome Robbins and Bob Fosse
OPENED: 11/29/56, New York; a run of 924 performances

Since appearing together in a nightclub revue, Comden and Green had wanted to write a musical for their friend, Judy Holliday. The idea they eventually hit upon was to cast Miss Holliday as a meddlesome operator at the Susanswerphone telephone answering service (a now out-of-date type of business later replaced by answering machines, voice mail and cell phones) who gets involved with her clients' lives. She is in fact so helpful to one, a playwright in need of inspiration, that they meet, fall in love (though through it all she conceals her occupation), dance and sing in the subway, and entertain fellow New Yorkers in Central Park. At last she confesses that she's the operator, and after some adjustment they happily couple up. Right before the happy conclusion, a dejected Ella exclaims "I'm Going Back," leaving Susanswerphone and her problems, and returning to her former job at the switchboard of the Bonjour Tristesse Brassiere Company in upstate New York. A film version, directed by Vincent Minelli, was made in 1960 that is virtually the stage show on film, with Dean Martin opposite Miss Holliday.

THE BEST LITTLE WHOREHOUSE IN TEXAS

MUSIC AND LYRICS: Carol Hall
BOOK: Larry King and Peter Masterson
DIRECTOR: Peter Masterson and Tommy Tune
CHOREOGRAPHER: Tommy Tune
OPENED: 6/19/78, New York; a run of 1,584 performances

The Chicken Ranch, a bordello in rural Texas, was a well attended institution for years. A friendly place, it derived its name from the fact that in the Depression clients were able to pay for their visits with poultry. This musical, based on the true story of the crusade by a conservative radio personality to shut down the Chicken Ranch, was brought to Broadway due to the efforts of Texans Carol Hall, Peter Masterson, Tommy Tune and Larry King—yes, *that* Larry King. Masterson was prompted to write the show after reading an article by King about the Chicken Ranch in a 1974 issue of *Playboy.* A surprisingly sweet and funny show, *The Best Little Whorehouse in Texas* immortalized the debate over the house, the rabid vigilante actions of the radio commentator Melvin P. Thorpe, and the two-faced politicians who publicly decried the institution, while privately being clients for many years. A sequel, *The Best Little Whorehouse Goes Public,* flopped on Broadway in 1994. A successful film was released in 1982, starring Dolly Parton and Burt Reynolds. Eventually evicted from the Chicken Ranch, the girls sing with worry and hope of their futures in "Hard Candy Christmas."

THE BOY FROM OZ

MUSIC AND LYRICS: Peter Allen
BOOK: Martin Sherman
DIRECTOR: Phillip William McKinley
CHOREOGRAPHER: Joey McKneely
OPENED: 3/5/98, Sidney
10/16/03, New York; a run of 364 performances

Australian-born Peter Allen was a quintessential 1970s performer, a rag to riches, Australian bush country to Radio City Music Hall story. This musical biography uses the songs that Allen wrote throughout his life, many of which were already autobiographical, to weave together the story of this flamboyant performer from meager beginnings, to marriage with Liza Minelli, to his own death of AIDS. "Don't Cry Out Loud" appears late in the show, sung by Peter's mother Marion. This ballad shows Peter's compulsion to hide his feelings deep within himself, while putting forward a flashy, untouchable personality outside. Drawing on the success of the Sydney production, *The Boy from Oz* came to Broadway in 2003 as a star vehicle for another Aussie, movie star Hugh Jackman.

CHESS

MUSIC: Benny Andersson and Björn Ulvaeus
LYRICS: Tim Rice
BOOK: Richard Nelson, based on an idea by Tim Rice
DIRECTOR: Trevor Nunn
CHOREOGRAPHER: Lynne Taylor-Corbett
OPENED: 5/14/86, London, closed 4/4/89
4/28/88, New York; a run of 68 performances

There have been musicals about the cold war (*Leave it to Me!, Silk Stockings*), but *Chess* was the first to treat the conflict seriously, using an international chess match as a metaphor. The idea originated with Tim Rice, who first tried to interest his former partner, Andrew Lloyd Webber, in the project. When that failed, he approached Andersson and Ulvaeus, writers and singers with the Swedish pop group AᗺBA. Like *Jesus Christ Superstar* and *Evita*, *Chess* originated as a successful concept album before it became a stage musical. The London production was a high-tech spectacle, rock opera type presentation. The libretto was revised for New York, and a different production approach was tried. It is ironic that the musical opened on Broadway at the tail end of the Cold War era, which may have made the subject matter seem less than current. The story is a romantic triangle with a Bobby Fischer type American chess champion, a Russian opponent who defects to the West, and the Hungarian born American, Florence, who transfers her affections from the American to the Russian without bringing happiness to anyone. Realizing early on the futility of her love for the Russian, Florence sings of her predicament in the ballad "Heaven Help My Heart."

CHICAGO

MUSIC: John Kander
LYRICS: Fred Ebb
BOOK: Fred Ebb and Bob Fosse
DIRECTION AND CHOREOGRAPHY: Bob Fosse
OPENED: 6/3/75, New York; a run of 936 performances

Based on Maureen Dallas Watkins' 1926 play *Roxie Hart*, this tough, flint-hearted musical tells the story of Roxie (Gwen Verdon), a married chorus girl who kills her faithless lover in gangster-ridden Chicago of the 1920s. She manages to win release from prison through the histrionic efforts of razzle-dazzle lawyer Billy Flynn (Jerry Orbach), and ends up as a vaudeville headliner with another "scintillating sinner," Velma Kelly (Chita Rivera), performing "Nowadays" every night. This scathing indictment of the American legal system, political system, media and morals may have been ahead of its time in its original 1975 production. It came roaring back for a spare and stylish smash 1996 revival Broadway revival, one of the longest running productions in Broadway history. A more lavish movie treatment, directed by Broadway choreographer Rob Marshall, was released in 2002, starring Renée Zellweger, Catherine Zeta-Jones, and Richard Gere in the lead roles. Against all odds for a new movie musical, it was a critical and popular hit. As soon as slick Billy Flynn agrees to take Roxie's case, her name is plastered all over the papers, and she is the talk of the town. This pleases her greatly, and fuels her self-delusion, as she sings in "Roxie."

A CHORUS LINE

MUSIC: Marvin Hamlisch
LYRICS: Edward Kleban
BOOK: James Kirkwood and Nicholas Dante
DIRECTOR: Michael Bennett
CHOREOGRAPHER: Michael Bennett and Bob Avian
OPENED: 7/25/75, New York; a run of 6,137 performances

Until overtaken by *Cats,* this musical stood for years as the longest-running show in Broadway history. It also won numerous Tony Awards, including Best Musical, plus the Pulitzer Prize for drama. The story is simple: seventeen dancers reveal their life stories as they audition for eight chorus parts in an unnamed Broadway musical. The show concentrates on the joys and troubles of their childhood and teen years. Cassie is singled out early by name, and we learn that she has already had success as a leading lady, when she was involved with producer Zach years before. Their love and her opportunities faded, and now she needs to start over again, even in the chorus, just for the chance to dance ("The Music and the Mirror").

ELEGIES FOR ANGELS, PUNKS AND RAGING QUEENS

MUSIC: Janet Hood
LYRICS AND BOOK: Bill Russell
DIRECTION AND STAGING: Bill Russell
OPENED: first performance 5/89, New York

Composer/lyricist Bill Russell was extremely moved when the Names Project Quilt was unveiled in Washington, DC in 1987, memorializing those dead from AIDS. A fan of the Edgar Lee Masters' collection of poems, *Spoon River Anthology*, where members in a cemetery recite their own epitaphs, Russell set out to create his own show, told in the words and stories of AIDS patients, which celebrates life and love, struggle and hope. The show, often given in conjunction with AIDS awareness and fundraising, has been performed in several countries, including the U.K., Germany, Sweden, Israel and Australia. A recording was made of the all-star performance given in New York in April, 2001, to benefit the Momentum AIDS Project. Some of the songs have a gospel feel to them, including the number "Angels, Punks and Raging Queens."

FOLLIES

MUSIC AND LYRICS: Stephen Sondheim
BOOK: James Goldman
DIRECTION: Harold Prince and Michael Bennett
CHOREOGRAPHER: Michael Bennett
OPENED: 4/4/71, New York; a run of 522 performances

Follies takes place at a reunion of former Ziegfeld Follies-type showgirls on the night before the destruction of the theatre where they all once played. The musical deals with the reality of life as contrasted with the unreality of the theatre and the past. *Follies* explores this theme through the lives of two couples, the upper-class, unhappy, Phyllis and Benjamin Stone, and the middle-class, also unhappy, Sally and Buddy Plummer. The show also shows us these four as they were in their pre-marital youth. The young actors appear as ghosts to haunt their elder selves. Because the show is about the past, and often in cinematically inspired flashback, Sondheim styled his songs to evoke some of the theatre's great composers and lyricists of the past. In a show of often melancholy recollections, former chorus girl and showbiz veteran Carlotta Campion is happy to have survived the good and bum times, singing "I'm Still Here." Since the show is set in 1971, Carlotta's survivor list includes many specific references to the 1920s through the 1950s.

THE FULL MONTY

MUSIC AND LYRICS: David Yazbek
BOOK: Terrence McNally
DIRECTOR: Jack O'Brien
CHOREOGRAPHER: Jerry Mitchell
OPENED: 10/26/00, New York; a run of 770 performances

Based on the successful British movie of the same name, *The Full Monty* was David Yazbek's first foray into Broadway. The scene for the stage musical is changed to Buffalo, New York. The men in the story are unemployed factory workers. Determined to support themselves and their families, the decidedly average group form a Chippendale's type strip act, baring everything (as the British phrase "the full monty" implies) for entertainment and cash. Each of the guys has a personal obstacle to overcome, and the act of stripping publicly becomes a symbol of freedom and pride, rather than the embarrassment it once seemed. Harold, a former factory manager, has not been able to admit to his wife Vicki that he has lost his job. They continue to keep up appearances, attending a dance-class regularly. In "Life with Harold" she mambos to the many ways she loves her doting husband.

GRAND HOTEL

MUSIC AND LYRICS: Maury Yeston; and Robert Wright and George Forrest
BOOK: Luther Davis
DIRECTOR AND CHOREOGRAPHER: Tommy Tune
OPENED: 11/12/89, New York; a run of 1,018 performances

Based on a novel by Vicki Baum, *Grand Hotel* interweaves the staff and guests at a posh Berlin hotel of c1930, just as the star-studded film of 1932 mixed the stories of Greta Garbo, Lionel Barrymore, Joan Crawford and a host of others. On Broadway, the stories included the penniless Baron's plans to steal the aging ballerina's jewels (he instead falls in love with her), the businessman who wrestles with his conscience, an aspiring actress who reluctantly peddles her flesh and the accountant with a zeal for living in the face of a fatal disease. The sub-plots intermingled and intersected predominantly through dance in the Tommy Tune production. Aspiring actress, but current typist, Flaemmchen confides to the girl in the mirror "I Want to Go to Hollywood."

GREASE

MUSIC, LYRICS AND BOOK: Jim Jacobs and Warren Casey
DIRECTOR: Tom Moore
CHOREOGRAPHER: Patricia Birch
OPENED: 2/14/72, New York; a run of 3,388 performances

A surprise runaway hit reflecting the nostalgia fashion of the 1970s, *Grease* is the story of hip greaser Danny Zuko and his wholesome girl Sandy Dumbrowski, a loose plot that serves as an excuse for a light-hearted ride through the early rock and roll of the 1950s. The 1978 movie version, starring John Travolta and Olivia Newton-John, is one of the top grossing movie musicals of all time. A hit revival opened in 1994, with a revolving Rizzo, played by Rosie O'Donnell, Brook Shields, Lucy Lawless and Debbie Gibson, among others. Tough girl Rizzo fears she might be pregnant. When consoled by chaste Sandy, Rizzo angrily lashes out at her, saying, "There Are Worse Things I Can Do."

HAIRSPRAY

MUSIC: Marc Shaiman
LYRICS: Scott Wittman and Marc Shaiman
BOOK: Mark O'Donnell and Thomas Meehan
DIRECTOR: Jack O'Brien
CHOREOGRAPHER: Jerry Mitchell
OPENED: 8/15/02, New York; still running as of December 2005

Film composer Marc Shaiman helped turn John Waters' campy 1988 movie *Hairspray* into perfect fodder for a new Broadway musical—teenage angst, racial integration, a lot of dancing and a whole lot of hair. Plump heroine Tracy Turnblad dreams of dancing on the Corny Collins TV show, but is upstaged by the prettier, but less talented, current "It-girl" Amber Von Tussle. Tracy envisions good things for herself, as she knows she can take down Amber in "I Can Hear the Bells." Amber has the support of her overbearing mother, Velma, who is also the producer for Corny Collins. Velma, a former child star, waxes poetic on her fame, and rages that Tracy will never reach the heights Velma did when she was "Miss Baltimore Crabs." Tracy eventually dances her way onto the show and gains acceptance for all teens of every size, shape and color.

I LOVE YOU, YOU'RE PERFECT, NOW CHANGE

MUSIC: Jimmy Roberts
LYRICS AND BOOK: Joe DiPietro
DIRECTOR: Joel Bishoff
OPENED: 8/1/95, New York; still running as of December 2005

This sleeper hit Off-Broadway revue addresses the whole messy process of being single, dating, finding romance, picking a mate, marrying, having children, having affairs, trying to rekindle the spark in marriage, etc. Though simple in its conception, the show found its niche as a good "date" musical, sailing past 3,000 performances in 2005, and seeing productions in cities around the world. A woman prepares for a date in "I Will Be Loved Tonight."

JESUS CHRIST SUPERSTAR

MUSIC: Andrew Lloyd Webber
LYRICS: Tim Rice
DIRECTOR: Tom O'Horgan
OPENED: 10/21/71, New York; a run of 711 performances

Through conceived as a theatre piece about the final week in the life of Jesus, the young team of Lloyd Webber and Rice could not find a producer interested in a "rock opera." Instead, they recorded it as an album, which became a smash hit. Concert tours of the show followed. It didn't take any more convincing that this would fly in the theatre. The concept of a "rock opera" caused quite a stir at the time. "I Don't Know How to Love Him" is Mary Magdalene's big ballad. In it she wrestles with how to deal with the emotions she feels for Jesus, and her own suddenly changed feelings about herself.

THE LAST FIVE YEARS

MUSIC: Jason Robert Brown
LYRICS AND BOOK: Jason Robert Brown
DIRECTOR: Daisy Prince
OPENED: 3/3/02, New York

The Off-Broadway musical *The Last Five Years* paired writer Jason Robert Brown and director Daisy Prince together again after their collaboration on the revue *Songs for a New World.* This two-person show chronicles the beginning, middle and deterioration of a relationship between a successful writer and a struggling actress. The show's form is unique. Cathy starts at the end of the relationship, and tells her story backwards, while Jamie starts at the beginning. The only point of intersection is the middle at their engagement. In "See I'm Smiling," Cathy senses the marriage is crumbling and tries to reconcile with Jamie one more time, but conversation dissolves into argument once again. The relationship has taken its toll on Cathy; she is "Still Hurting" after the break-up (the show's opening song), wondering about the love and the lies that Jamie gave her. The two original actors Off-Broadway were Norbert Leo Butz and Sherie René Scott.

THE LION KING

MUSIC: Elton John
LYRICS: Tim Rice
BOOK: Roger Allers and Irene Mecchi
DIRECTOR: Julie Taymor
CHOREOGRAPHER: Garth Fagan
OPENED: 11/13/97, New York; still running as of December 2005

A fantastic triumph of art design and choreography, Julie Taymor's adaptation to the stage of the 1994 Disney movie won both critical and popular praise. Lavish sets and costumes, including actors on stilts, set this production high above other movie-to-stage adaptations. The Broadway score incorporates all the music from the original movie, along with new material. Mufasa, king of the lions, is murdered by his brother Scar. Young Simba is led to believe he killed his father and runs away to exile. As an adult, Simba returns to overthrow the evil Scar and claim his birthright as king. Childhood friend and fellow lion Nala stays, and endures the evil Scar's reign over the pride. She decides she can no longer bear her circumstances, and must pass into the jungle to find a new life in "Shadowland."

MONTY PYTHON'S SPAMALOT

MUSIC: John Du Prez and Eric Idle
LYRICS: Eric Idle
BOOK: Eric Idle, "lovingly ripped off" from the motion picture *Monty Python and the Holy Grail*
DIRECTOR: Mike Nichols
CHOREOGRAPHER: Casey Nicholaw
OPENED: 3/17/05, New York, still running as of December 2005

Eric Idle, one of the founding members of the British television comedy troupe "Monty Python's Flying Circus," made his Broadway writing debut with *Monty Python's Spamalot*, billed as "a new musical lovingly ripped off from the motion picture *Monty Python and the Holy Grail*." As in the movie, the show involves the wacky adventures of King Arthur and his band of knights in their search for the Holy Grail, shrubbery, and in the musical, success on the Great White Way. The lavish *Spamalot* was directed by luminary Broadway and movie director Mike Nichols. The original cast starred Tim Curry, Hank Azaria, and David Hyde Pierce. True to characteristic Python irreverence and silliness, *Spamalot* lambasts the musical genre at every step, one such example being "Whatever Happened to My Part?" where the Lady of the Lake wonders why she is underused in the second act.

THE PRODUCERS

MUSIC AND LYRICS: Mel Brooks
BOOK: Mel Brooks and Thomas Meehan
DIRECTOR/CHOREOGRAPHER: Susan Stroman
OPENED: 4/19/01, New York; still running as of December 2005

Mel Brooks swept critics and audiences off their feet in New York with this show, adapted from his 1968 movie *The Producers*. A couple songs from the movie were incorporated into the otherwise new stage score. The story concerns washed-up Broadway producer Max Bialystock and his nerdy accountant Leo Bloom, who has dreams of being a producer himself. During an audit of Max's books, Leo offhandedly remarks that one could make more money producing a flop than a hit. The two eventually produce the show "Springtime for Hitler," which seems on paper like it will be the biggest flop ever. It's a surprise hit and Bialystock and Bloom are in trouble. All ends well, after a brief prison detour. Svelte, sexy Swede Ulla comes to the offices of Bialystock and Bloom to audition (she is hired as secretary), her only talent being "When You Got It, Flaunt It." The original cast included Broadway stars Nathan Lane (Max) and Matthew Broderick (Leo). The director and most of the lead actors from Broadway were in the 2005 movie musical.

SONGS FOR NEW WORLD

MUSIC AND LYRICS: Jason Robert Brown
DIRECTOR: Daisy Prince
CHOREOGRAPHER: Michael Arnold
OPENED: 10/26/95, New York; a run of 27 performances

In 1994, Daisy Prince, daughter of Broadway legend Harold Prince, went to hear a 24-year-old Greenwich Village coffeehouse pianist named Jason Robert Brown play some of his original compositions. A collaboration and a friendship were born when she heard he was working on a concert evening of songs that played like offbeat short stories. Titled *Songs for a New World*, the piece was developed at a summer festival in Toronto. Musically distinctive and precocious, the songs look at contemporary life from unusual angles. In the plotless, Off-Broadway revue, a shrill wife at the end of her rope, unloved and cheated on, threatens her husband from a high ledge. She'll end it all with "Just One Step"—just you watch!

A STAR IS BORN (film)

MUSIC: Harold Arlen
LYRICS: Ira Gershwin
SCREENPLAY: William Wellman, Dorothy Parker, Alan Cambell, Moss Hart
DIRECTOR: George Cukor
CHOREOGRAPHER: Richard Barstow
RELEASED: 1954, Warner Bros.

This movie musical about the rise and fall in show business chronicles the alcoholic, waning star Norman Maine (James Mason) and his new romance, the ascending showgirl Esther Blodgett (Judy Garland). Esther's career as a musical movie star wins her an Oscar, while Norman hits the skids. Though they love one another, his self-destruction takes over and he drowns himself. Judy Garland belts out many show stoppers in her big comeback movie, a few years after being fired from MGM. Early in the story, she sings "The Man that Got Away" in an after-hours rehearsal in a nightclub, overheard by movie star Norman. The Gershwin/Arlen torch song became a signature Garland number. Two other movies have been made using the same storyline but different music; a 1937 version, and the 1976 star vehicle for Barbra Streisand.

THOROUGHLY MODERN MILLIE

MUSIC: Jeanine Tesori
LYRICS: Dick Scanlan
BOOK: Dick Scanlan and Richard Morris
DIRECTOR: Michael Mayer
CHOREOGRAPHER: Rob Ashford
OPENED: 4/18/02, New York; a run of 903 performances

Based on the 1967 movie starring Julie Andrews, *Thoroughly Modern Millie* is a new musical, retaining only three of the songs from the movie (including the title song), with a score by Jeanine Tesori. It chronicles the life of Millie, a transplanted Kansas girl trying to make it big in New York in the flapper days of the 1920s. She stays at the Hotel Priscilla, along with other young starlets, which is run by the sinister Mrs. Meers, who actually is running a white slave trade on the side. The madcap plot has many twists and turns, and shows a cheery slice of life in New York during the Jazz age. Millie decides in the end that it is only love she is interested in. She belts this sentiment high and loud in "Gimme Gimme."

WICKED

MUSIC AND LYRICS: Stephen Schwartz
BOOK: Winnie Holzman, based on the novel "Wicked: The Life and Times of the Wicked Witch of the West" by Gregory Maguire
DIRECTOR: Joe Mantello
CHOREOGRAPHER: Wayne Cilento
OPENED: 10/30/03, New York; still running as of December 2005

Stephen Schwartz's return to Broadway came with *Wicked,* a hit from 2003. Based on Gregory Maguire's 1995 book, the musical chronicles the backstory of the Wicked Witch of the West, Elphaba, and Good Witch of the North, Glinda (Galinda), before their story threads are picked up in L. Frank Baum's *The Wonderful Wizard of Oz.* At times a dark show, the original production was characterized by lavish sets and a stellar cast, including Kristin Chenoweth, Idina Menzel, Norbert Leo Butz, and Broadway immortal Joel Grey. The two witches first cross paths back in school as unlikely roommates. Elphaba, shy, and green, learns from radiant Galinda just what it takes to be "Popular." Feeling unloved and left out, Elphaba laments her fate in "I'm Not that Girl." Ignored by her own father, Elphaba envisions a strong relationship with the Wizard, and a new exciting life for herself in "The Wizard and I."

THE WILD PARTY

MUSIC, LYRICS AND BOOK: Andrew Lippa
DIRECTOR: Gabriel Barre
CHOREOGRAPHER: Mark Dendry
OPENED: 2/24/00, New York; a run of 54 performances

Two productions of *The Wild Party* hit New York in 2000, the unsuccessful Broadway show by Michael John LaChiusa, and the Off-Broadway, and now more popular Andrew Lippa musical. Both were based on the scandalous 1928 poem by *The New Yorker* editor Joseph Moncure March. This jazz age drama, depicting a night of decadence and debauchery at a party thrown by lusty showgirl Queenie and her abusive lover, vaudeville clown Burrs, was inspiration for Lippa's accomplished score. Kate, a semi-reformed hooker, arrives with her squeeze, Mr. Black. She belts of her humble beginnings in "Look at Me Now." After the wanton night of excessive partying and drama, Queenie surveys the scene in "How Did We Come to This?" to end the show.

WISH YOU WERE HERE

MUSIC AND LYRICS: Harold Rome
BOOK: Arthur Kober and Joshua Logan
DIRECTOR AND CHOREOGRAPHER: Joshua Logan
OPENED: 6/25/52, New York; a run of 598 performances

It was known as the musical with the swimming pool, but *Wish You Were Here* had other things going for it, including a cast full of ingratiating performers, a warm and witty score by Harold Rome, and a director who wouldn't stop making improvements even after the Broadway opening (among them were new dances choreographed by Jerome Robbins). The musical was adapted by Arthur Kober and Joshua Logan from Kober's own play, *Having a Wonderful Time*, and is about a group of middle-class New Yorkers trying to make the most of a two-week vacation at an adult summer camp in the mountains (of upstate New York or New England). "Shopping Around" is an outrageous number sung by vampy Fay, who will find what she wants, trying out one man at a time.

WONDERFUL TOWN

MUSIC: Leonard Bernstein
LYRICS: Betty Comden and Adolph Green
BOOK: Joseph A. Fields and Jerome Chodorov
DIRECTOR: George Abbott
CHOREOGRAPHER: Donald Saddler
OPENED: 2/25/53, New York; a run of 559 performances

Wonderful Town reunited the creative team that made 1944's *On the Town* so successful: Bernstein, Comden and Green, and director George Abbott. Set in New York, this show is not a sequel; rather it is based on the hit Broadway play *My Sister Eileen*, which itself was based on Ruth McKinney's semi-autobiographical *New Yorker* short stories. The musical was conceived as a showcase for Rosiland Russell as Ruth. Ruth and Eileen are two sisters making their way in Greenwich Village, originally from a small town in Ohio. Ruth is a writer, and Eileen is…well, pretty. The tomboyish, assertive Ruth describes her failures at dating in "One Hundred Easy Ways to Lose a Man." As Ruth chases the story, Eileen is chased by suitor after suitor. Ruth's editor, Bob Baker, comes over to apologize for being curt with Ruth, and Eileen immediately falls "a little bit in love" with him. After a raucous night with seven amorous, Conga-dancing Brazilian naval cadets that lands Eileen in jail, all is well in the end as she realizes that Ruth and Bob love one another, and Eileen finds a singing career.
A revival came to Broadway in 2002, with Donna Murphy as Ruth.

THE PAST IS ANOTHER LAND

from Elton John and Tim Rice's *Aida*

Music by ELTON JOHN
Lyrics by TIM RICE

Gently, moderately

E5
E(♭5)(no3rd)
E5
E(♭5)(no3rd)
E5
A/E
E
sess
The past is now an - oth - er land
p
8vb
8vb
B/E
A/E
E
G#7
C#
far be-yond my reach
In - vad - ed by in - sid-ious for - eign
F#
B
E/D
A/C#
bod - ies for-eign speech
Where the time - less joys of child - hood
Lie
mf
E/B
Bsus
B
E
F#/E
E
F#/E
E
F#/E
E
F#/E
bro - ken on the beach
The
p
p

E5
A/E
E5
B/E
A/E
E5
pres - ent is an emp - ty space Be-tween the good and bad A
p
G#7/D#
C#sus
C#
F#
B
mo - ment lead - ing no - where Too point - less to be sad But
E5/D
A/C#
E5/B
B5
E5
E(♭5)(no3rd)
time e-nough to lay to waste Ev-'ry cer - tain-ty I had
E
E(♭5)(no3rd)
E
E(♭5)(no3rd)
E
E5
colla voce
A5/E
E5
The fu - ture is a bar - ren world from
poco cresc.
sub. p
rit.
subito

A tempo
B5/E
A5/E
E5
G♯7/D♯
C♯sus
C♯
which I can't re - turn Both heart - less and_ ma - ter - i - al Its
F♯sus
F♯
Bsus
B
E/D
A/C♯
wretch - ed spoils_ not my con - cern_ Shin - ing like an e - vil sun As my
Bsus
B
E(add2)
E/D
colla voce
A/C♯
child - hood treas - ures burn Shin - ing like an e - vil sun As my
rall.
sub. p
Bsus
B
E5
E(♭5)(no3rd)
E5
E(♭5)(no3rd)
E5
E(♭5)(no3rd)
child hood treas ures burn.
pp
8vb

I KNOW THE TRUTH

from Elton John and Tim Rice's *Aida*

Music by ELTON JOHN
Lyrics by TIM RICE

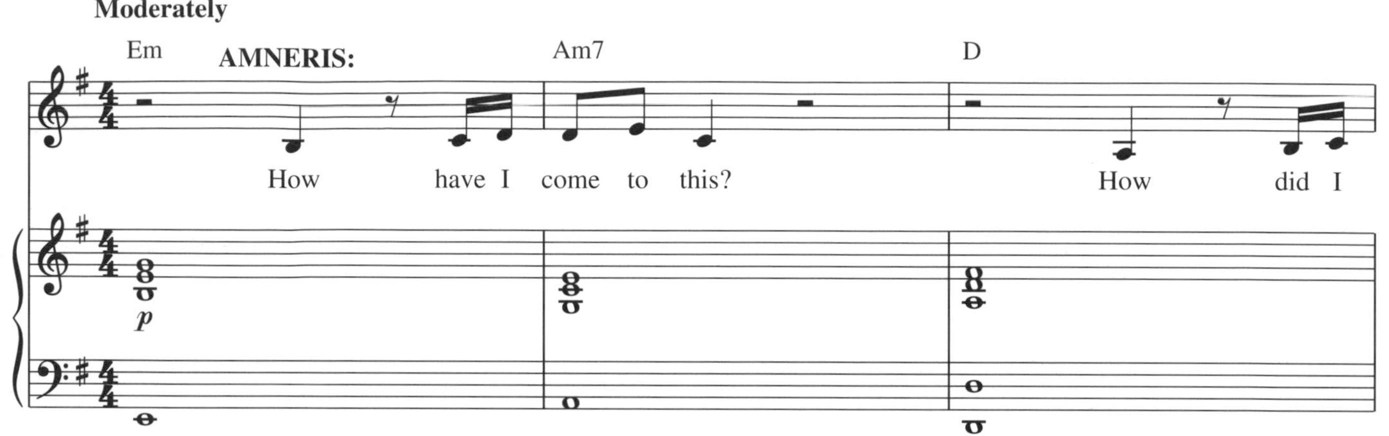

Am7
D
G
G6
been my time It's o - ver it nev - er be - gan
C/E
D
I closed my eyes to so much for so long and I no
G
C/G
G
F/A
G/B
long - er can I try to blame it on
C
D
Bm
for - tune Somekind of shift in a star

Em
Am7
D
But I know the truth and it haunts me It's flown just a lit - tle too
G
F/A
G/B
C
far I know the truth and it mocks me
D
Bsus
B
I know the truth and it shocks me
Em
Am7
Cmaj7/D
D
It's flown just a lit - tle too

C/G
G
D/F#
Em
far
Why do I
p
Am7
D7sus
D
G
want him still?
Why when there's noth-ing there?
C/E
D
G
C/G
How to go on with the rest of my life
To pre-tend I don't care?
G
Em
Am7
This should have been my time
It's

D
G
C/E
o - ver it nev - er be - gan
I closed my eyes to so
D
G
F/A
G/B
much for so long and I no long - er can
I try to blame it on
C
D
Bm
for - tune
Some kind of twist in my fate
Em
Am7
D
But I know the truth and it haunts me
I learned it a lit - tle too

G
F/G
G
C
late
I know the truth _ and it mocks me ___
f
8vb
D/C
Bsus
B
Em
I know the truth _ and it shocks me ________ I
rall.
Rubato
Am7
Dsus
D
Csus2
Gmaj7/B
learned it ____________ a lit - tle too late ___
C(add2)
D
G(add2)
Too late ________________________________

I GOT LOST IN HIS ARMS

from *Annie Get Your Gun*

Words and Music by
IRVING BERLIN

Con anima
mp
lost in his arms and I had to stay. It was
dark in his arms and I lost my way, From the
dark came a voice and it seemed to say, "There you
go, There you go." How I

felt as I fell I just can't re - call. But his arms held me
mp
fast and it broke the fall. And I said to my heart as it
fool - ish - ly kept jump - ing all a - round, "I got
lost, but look what I found."
ff
Ped.
*

THERE'S A FINE, FINE LINE

from the Broadway Musical *Avenue Q*

Music and Lyrics by ROBERT LOPEZ
and JEFF MARX

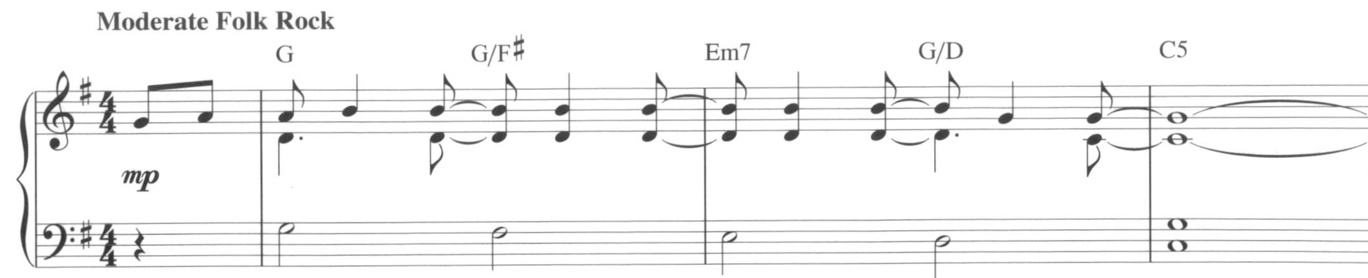

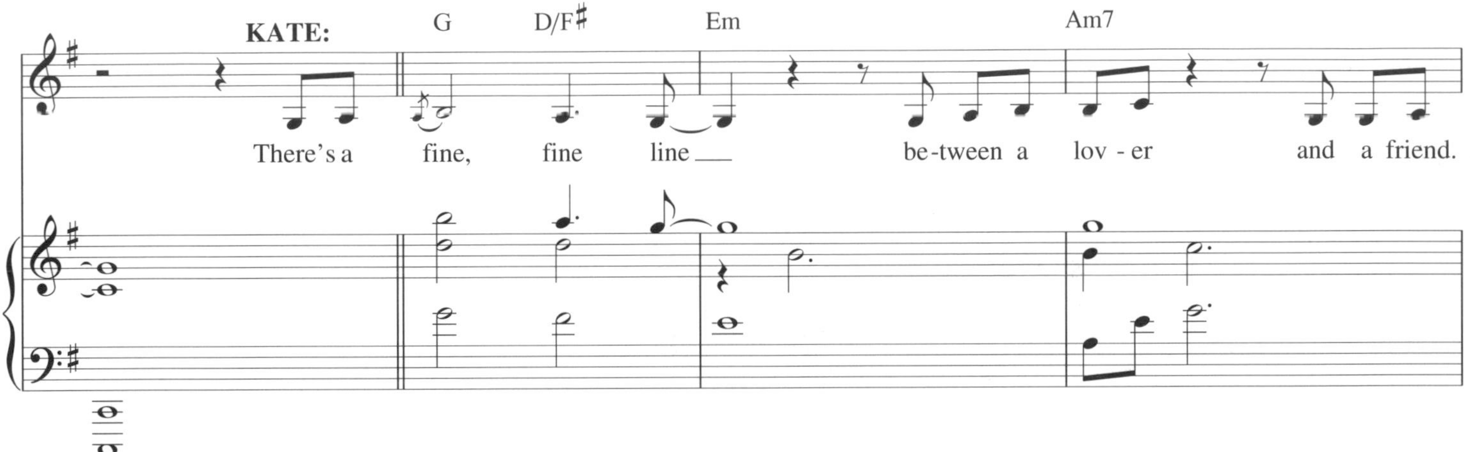

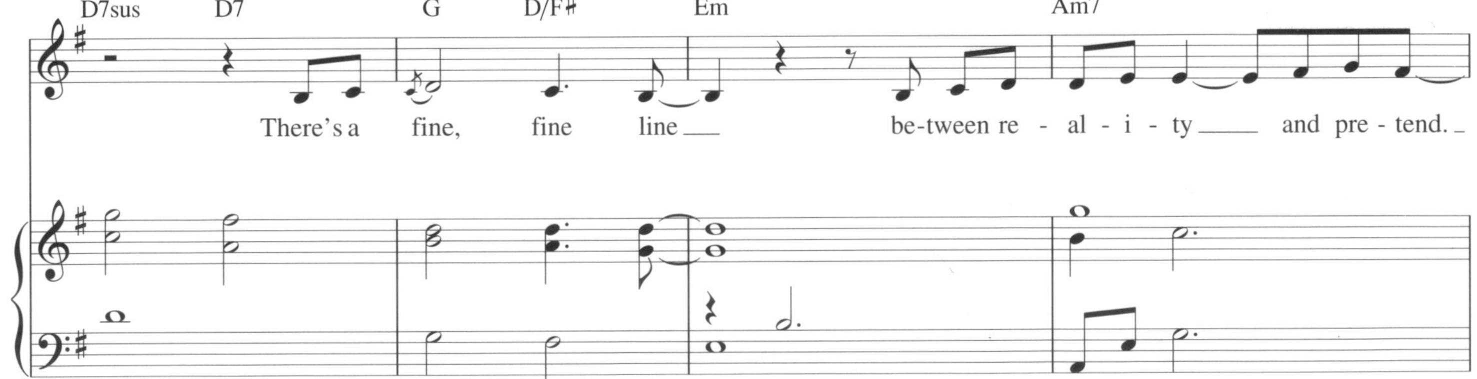

For more info about Avenue Q, visit www.AvenueQ.com

Cm G D/F♯ Em7 G/D Cmaj7
There's a fine, fine line be - tween love
D7sus G G/B Cmaj7 D5 G D/F♯
and a waste of time. There's a fine, fine line
8vb
Em Am7 D7sus D7 G D/F♯
be-tween a fair-y tale and a lie. And there's a fine, fine line
Em Am7 D7sus D7 G D/F♯
be-tween "you're won-der-ful" and "good-bye." I guess if some-one does - n't love

Em7
Bm7/D
Cmaj7
Cm
G
D/F♯
you back, it is-n't such a crime, but there's a fine, fine line
8vb
Em7
G/D
Cmaj7
D7sus
G
G/B
be - tween love and a waste of your time.
Cmaj7
D
D/C
G/B
And I don't have the time to waste on you an-y-more.
cresc.
f
8vb
G D Em7 D A/C♯
D
G
I don't think that you e - ven know what you're look-ing for.
8vb

G D/F♯ Em7 D E
E/D
C♯m7
For my own san - i - ty, I've got to close the door
8vb
F♯m F♯m/E
D
D7/C
Bm
and walk a - way...
Whoa...
dim.
mp
dim.
mp
D7(no3)
G D/F♯
Em
Am7
There's a fine, fine line be-tween to - geth - er and not.
D7sus D7
G D/F♯
Em
3
Am7
And there's a fine, fine line be-tween what you want-ed and what you

D
C/D
D
G
G/F♯
got.
You got - ta go af - ter the things
Em7
G/D
Cmaj7
Cm
E♭
F/E♭
E♭
you want while you're still in your prime...
F/E♭
F
Broader
G
G/F♯
Em7
G/D
C
Cmaj7
There's a fine, fine line be-tween love
rit.
8vb
poco rit.
8vb
D7(no3)
G
G/B
Cmaj7
D7
G
and a waste of time.
rit.
8vb

ANYTHING BUT LONELY

from *Aspects of Love*

Music by ANDREW LLOYD WEBBER
Lyrics by DON BLACK and CHARLES HART

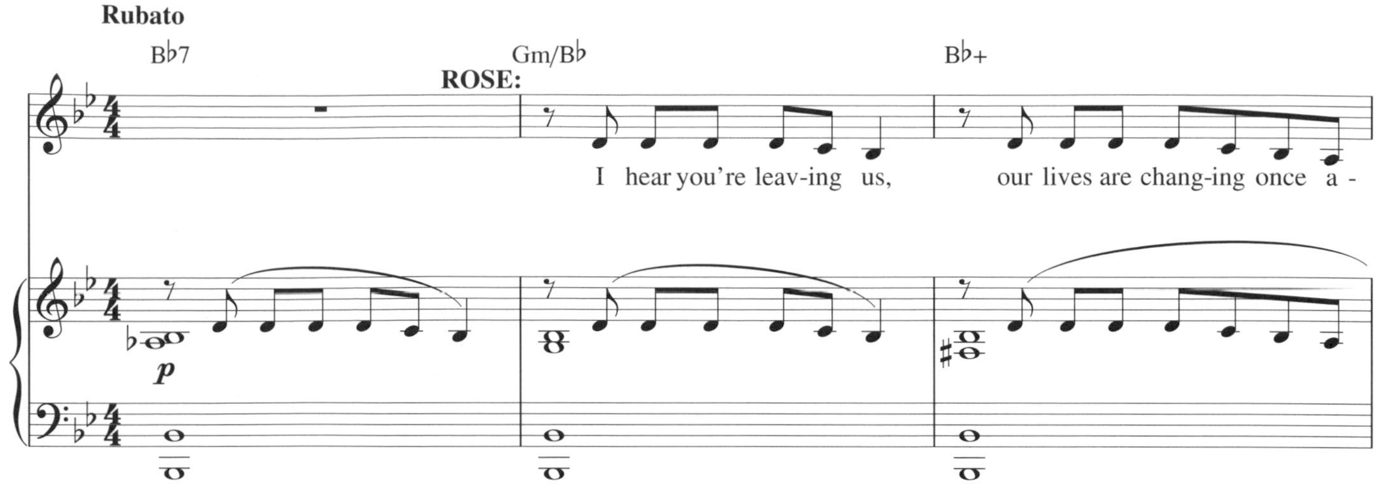

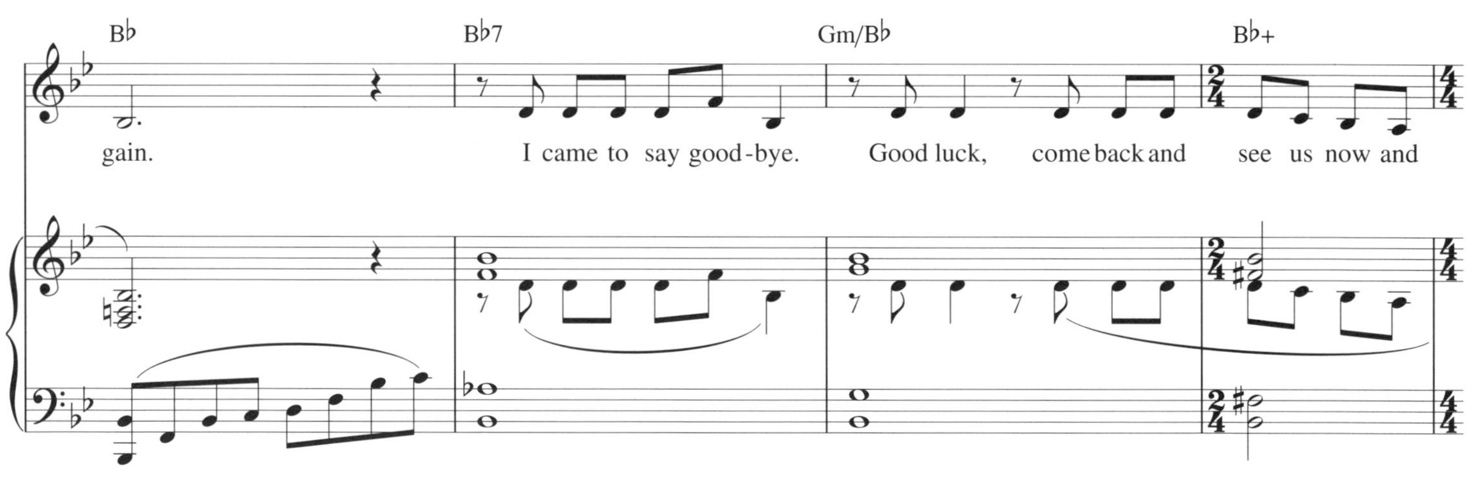

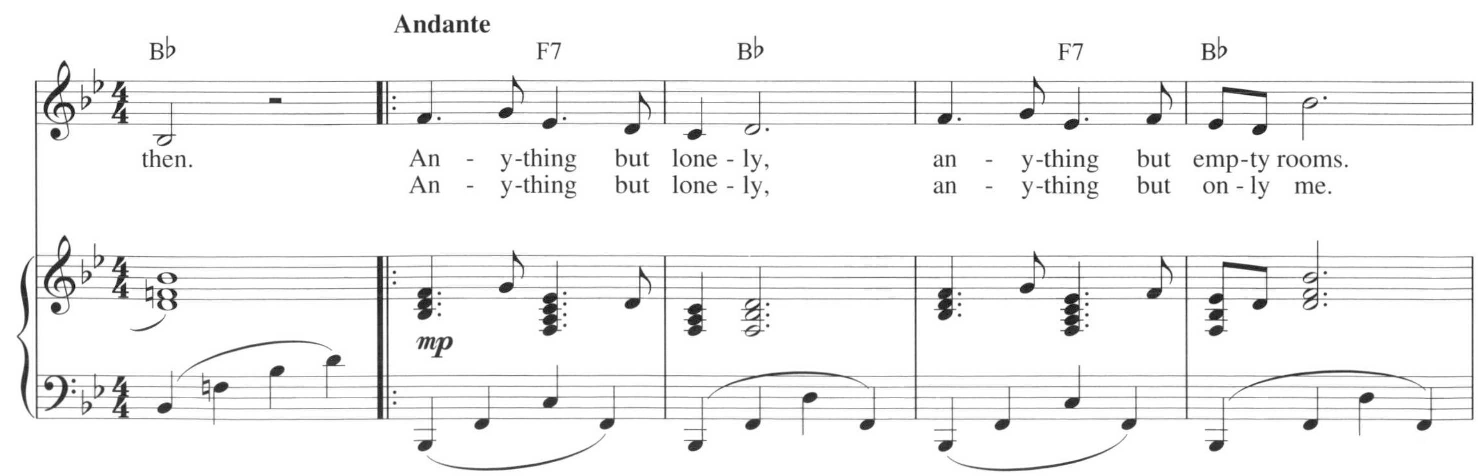

Dm/A Gm Cm/E♭ B♭/F F F7 B♭
There's so much in life to share– what's the sense when no one else is there?
Qui - et years in too much space– that's the thing that's hard to face, and...
B♭7 Gm/B♭ B♭+
You have a right to go, but you should al - so know that I won't be a - lone for
B♭ B♭7 Gm/B♭
long. Long days with noth - ing said are not what lie a - head–
B♭+ B♭ F7/B♭ B♭
I'm sor - ry but I'm not that strong. An - y - thing but lone - ly,
più f

F7/B♭
B♭
Dm/A
Gm
Cm/E♭
an - y-thing but pass-ing time.
Lone - ly's what I'll nev - er be,
B♭/F
F
F7
B♭7
Gm/B♭
while there's still some life in me, and...
I'm still young, don't for-get,
it is - n't o - ver yet–
B♭+
B♭
B♭7
so man - y hearts for me to thrill.
If you're not here to say
Gm/B♭
B♭+
B♭
how good I look each day,
I'll have to find some-one who will...
cresc.

B
F#7/B
B
F#7/B
B
An - y-thing but lone - ly,
an - y-thing but emp - ty rooms.
f
F#/A#
G#m
Em6
B/F#
F#
F#7
There's so much in life to share–
what's the sense when no one else is
B7
G#m/B
B/F#
there?
What's the sense when
F#7
B
F#7/B
B
no one else is there?
rall.
a tempo

I'M GOING BACK
from *Bells Are Ringing*

Words by BETTY COMDEN
and ADOLPH GREEN
Music by JULE STYNE

Bras - siere Com - pa - ny.
They've got a
great big switch-board there
Where it's just "Hel - lo, good - bye."
It may be dull,
But there I can be
just
me, my - self and I.
A lit - tle mod-'ling on the side

Yes, that's where I'll be at the
Bon - jour Tris - tesse Bras - siere Com-pa - ny.
And if an - y - bod - y asks for El - la, Me - la or Mom,
tell them that I'm go - ing back where I came from, to the B. T. Bras - si - ère

Com-pa - ny.
Free
Good - bye, ev - 'ry - bod - y; good - bye, Ma - dame Grim - al - di;
Broad and steady (Sarah Vaughn style)
good-bye, Jun - ior Mal - let, San - ta Claus is hit - tin' the road;
Lis - ten to your ma - ma, ma - ma, ma - ma. Eat your spin - ach, ba - by,

Valse Francaise (in three)
Eat your spin - ach, ba - by, by the load.
(Spoken:) La Petite Bergère Restaurant…
…adieu. Je ne reviendrai Jamais, jamais, jamais. C'est
tous fini, Adieu to yieu. So, (Sung:) Good - bye, Max, To your dogs and your
Allegro
cats, To the Duke of Wind - sor and his Duch - ess.

Good - bye, Bar - ton, Kit - chell and Has - tings. At last you're
out of my clutch - es. I'll miss you, but you'll car - ry
Slow
f-p
on. You'll nev - er know that I'm gone.
In tempo (with great energy, like a jazzy strut)
mp
I'm go - ing back where I can be

me,
To the Bon - jour Tris - tesse
Bras - siere Com-pa - ny.
And
while I'm sit - tin' there I hope that I'll find out
Just what El - la Pe - ter - son is
all a - bout,
In that Shang - ri - la of lac - y lin - ger - ie,
mf

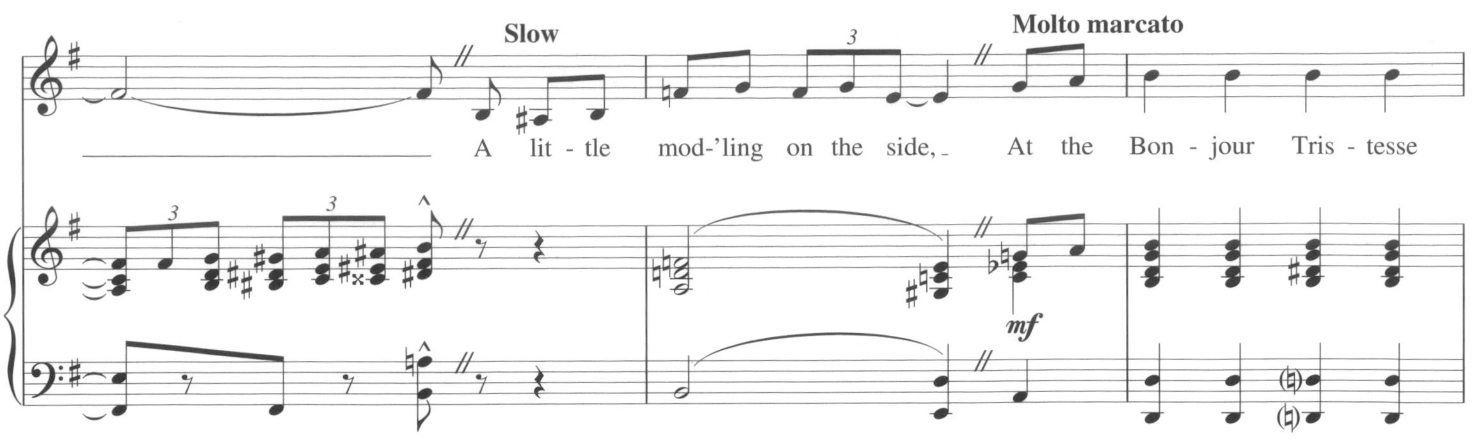
Slow
Molto marcato
A lit - tle mod-'ling on the side, At the Bon - jour Tris - tesse
mf

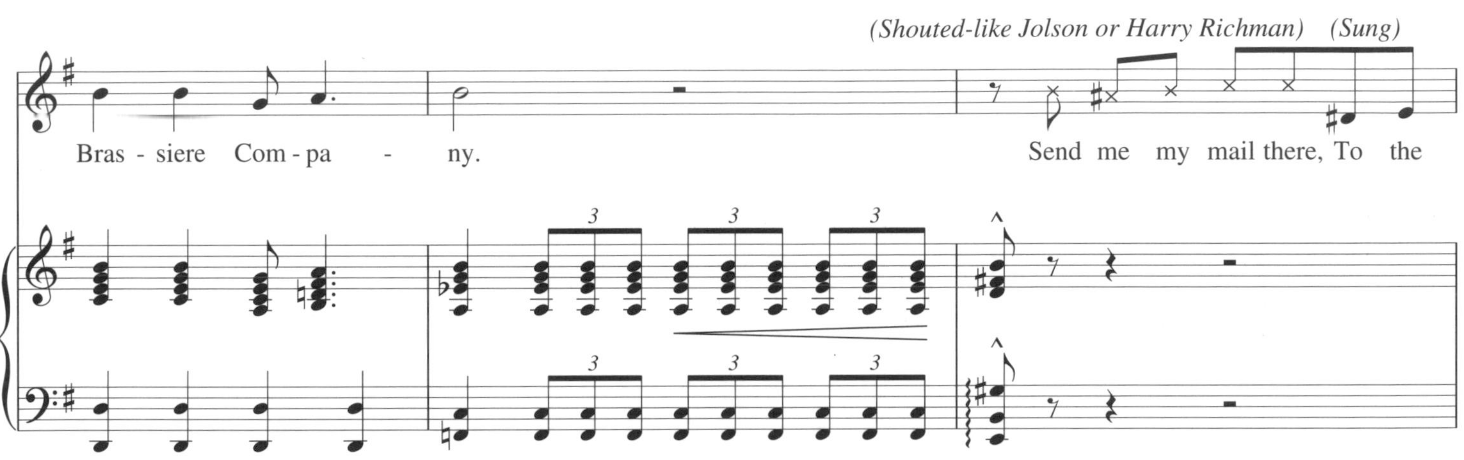
(Shouted-like Jolson or Harry Richman) (Sung)
Bras - siere Com - pa - ny.
Send me my mail there, To the

Bon - jour Tris - tesse Com - pa - ny.
f
ff

HARD CANDY CHRISTMAS

from *The Best Little Whorehouse in Texas*

Words and Music by
CAROL HALL

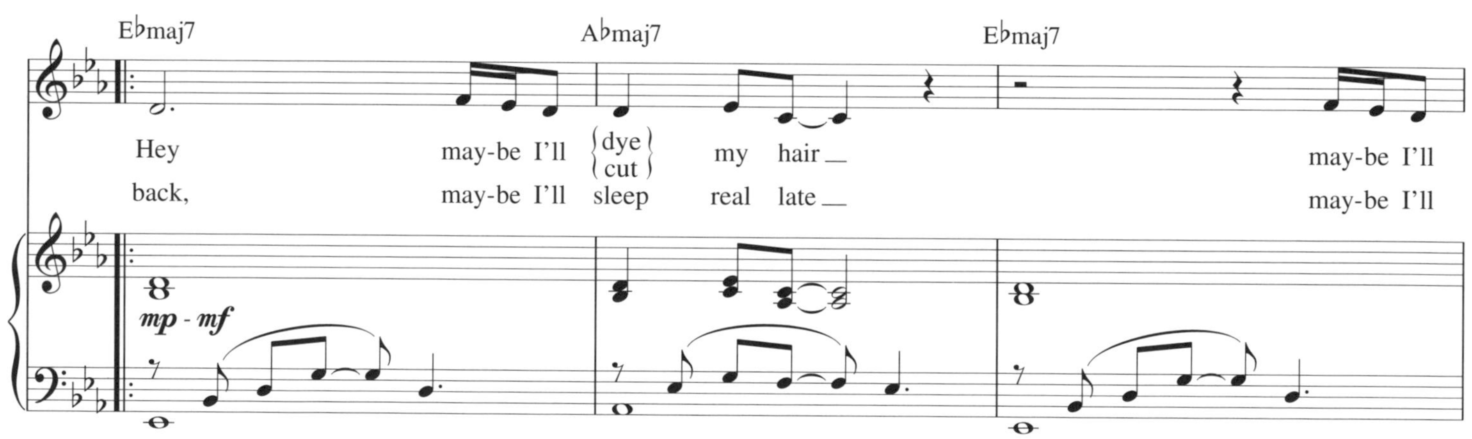

C
Fm7
B♭7
E♭maj7
A♭
track.
wine.
Me, I'll bounce right
Me, I'll be just
fine
fine
and dan - dy.
Lord, it's like a

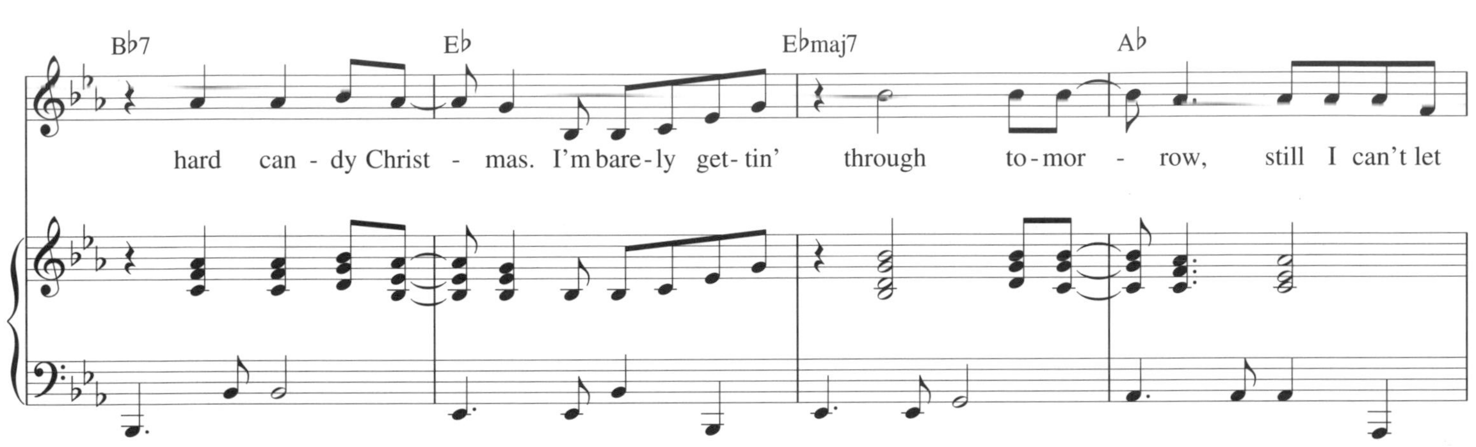
B♭7
E♭
E♭maj7
A♭
hard can - dy Christ - mas. I'm bare - ly get - tin' through to - mor - row, still I can't let

B♭7
1
E♭
2
E♭maj7
A♭
sor - row bring me way down.
I'll be

E♭maj7
A♭
Fm
B♭

C
Fm
B♭7(add13)
E♭maj7
A♭maj7
Hey
may-be I'll
up and go
learn to sew
on
may-be I'll
set - tle down
E♭maj7
A♭maj7
Fm7
may-be I'll just lie low may-be I'll hit the bars may-be I'll
may-be I'll just leave town may-be I'll have some fun may-be I'll
B♭7
C
Fm7
B♭7
E♭maj7
count the stars un - til the dawn.
Me, I will go
meet some-one and make him mine.
Me, I'll be just fine and dan -
A♭
B♭7
E♭
E♭maj7
- dy. Lord, it's like a hard can - dy Christ - mas. I'm bare-ly get-tin' through to-mor -

A♭
B♭7
E♭
E♭maj7
- row, still I can't let sor-row bring me way down. _ I'll be _ fine and dan -
A♭
B♭7
E♭
E♭maj7
- dy. Lord, it's like a hard can - dy Christ - mas. I'm bare-ly get-tin' through to-mor -
A♭
B♭7
E♭maj7
A♭maj7
E♭maj7
- row, still I can't let sor-row bring me way down. _ I'll be _ fine.
A♭maj7
E♭maj7
A♭maj7
E♭maj7
I'll be _ fine. I'll be _ fine. _

DON'T CRY OUT LOUD
(We Don't Cry Out Loud)
from *The Boy from Oz*

Words and Music by PETER ALLEN
and CAROLE BAYER SAGER

mf
know a lot a - bout her 'cause you see,
mf
Steadily
mf
ba - by is an aw - ful lot like me.
Don't cry out loud.
rall.
mf a tempo
Just keep it in - side, learn how to hide our feel - ings.
Fly high and proud, and if you should fall, re - mem-ber you
3
8vb

al-most had it all.
mp
mf
Spoken: Whatever goes on inside us is nobody's business. It's private.
Don't you ever forget that.
Re-mem-ber you al - most had it.
Don't cry out loud just keep it in - side learn how to
f
8vb

3
hide our feel-ings Fly high and proud, and if you should
fall re-mem-ber you al - most had it all,
cantabile
rall.
you al - most had it all.
mf
rall.
mf
mf
a tempo
mp
mp a tempo
rit.
mf
pp

OUR KIND OF LOVE

from *The Beautiful Game*

Music by ANDREW LLOYD WEBBER
Lyrics by BEN ELTON

Dm
G
C/E
G
Dm
Em/G
C
I must be bold - er.
Cling to my dream and nev - er tire.
C
Am
Dm
G
C/E
G
Each love de - nied,
leaves peo - ple cold - er.
New love re - kind - les
Dm
Em/G
C
C
G
Dm
Em/G
C
ev - 'ry fire.
I shan't be - tray my heart's de - sire.
Fsus4
F
F
C
G/B
Am
D9
Ev - en though we come from diff - 'rent sides.
We won't

G7sus4 G C Am Dm G
hide. I am in love, no one can blame me.
C/E G Dm Em/G C C Am
Such is my sto - ry and my fate. My kind of love,
Dm G C/E G Dm Em/G
will nev - er shame me. My love is strong - er than their
C C G Dm Em/G C
hate. My love is strong - er than their hate.

B♭
Gm
Cm
F
B♭/D
F
Cm
Dm/F
B♭
B♭
F
Cm
Dm/F
B♭
E♭sus4
E♭
E♭
B♭
B♭
B♭/A
I shall cling to him with all my might.
Gm
C9
E♭6/F
A♭7
It's my right.

Db
Bbm
Ebm
Ab7
Db/F
All kinds of love, bring us to - geth - er. Cau - ses the
Ab
Ebm
Fm/Ab
Db
Db
Bbm
bro - ken hearts to mend. Peo - ple must love,
Ebm
Ebm/Ab
Ab
Db/F
Ab
Ebm
Fm/Ab
now and for - ev - er. There's on - ly one love in the
Db
Db
Ab
Ebm
Fm/Ab
Db
end. There's on - ly one love in the end.

NOWADAYS
from *Chicago*

Words by FRED EBB
Music by JOHN KANDER

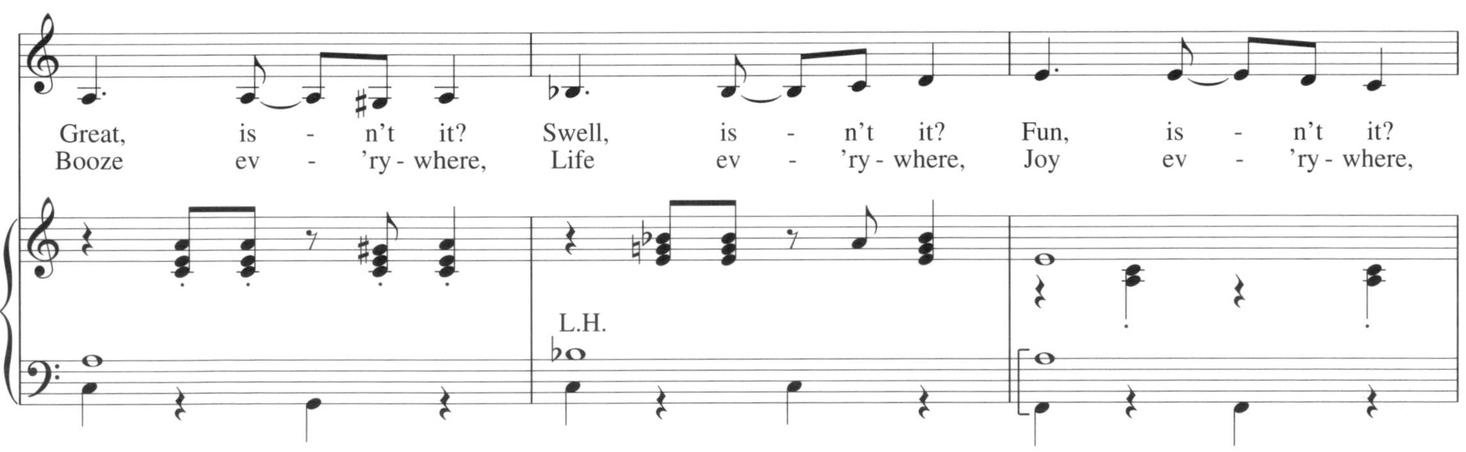

This song is a duet for Velma and Roxie in the show, adapted here as a solo.

2
Now - a - days.
You can
mf
like the life you're liv - ing. You can live the life you
mf
like. You can e - ven mar - ry Har - ry, but
mess a - round with Ike. And that's good, is - n't it?

Grand, is - n't it? Great, is - n't it? Swell. is - n't it?
Fun, is - n't it? But noth-ing stays. In fif - ty
years or so it's gon - na change you know. But oh, it's
heav - en now - a - days.
mf
f
ff
sfz

ROXIE
from *Chicago*

Words by FRED EBB
Music by JOHN KANDER

E♭m
B♭7
E♭m
leb - ri - ty. that means some-bod - y ev - 'ry - one knows.
3
C7
Fm
D♭7 B(add2)/E♭ Em6 D♭7/F
They're gon - na rec - og - nize my eyes, my hair, my teeth, my
cresc.
G♭m E/G E/G♯ D♭7 N.C.
G♭
boobs, my nose.
From just some
mf
E♭/G
A♭m7
D♭7
dumb mech - an - ic's wife I'm gon - na be Rox - ie.

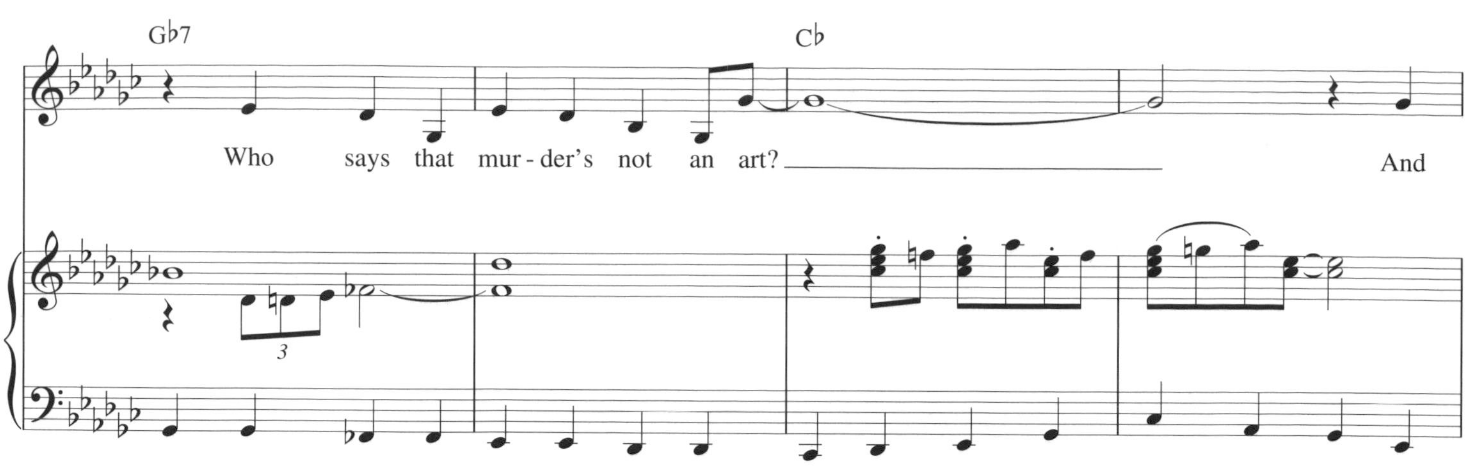
Gb7
Cb
Who says that mur-der's not an art?
And

D7#11
Gb/Db
Ab9
who in case she does-n't hang
can say she start-ed with a bang?
cresc.

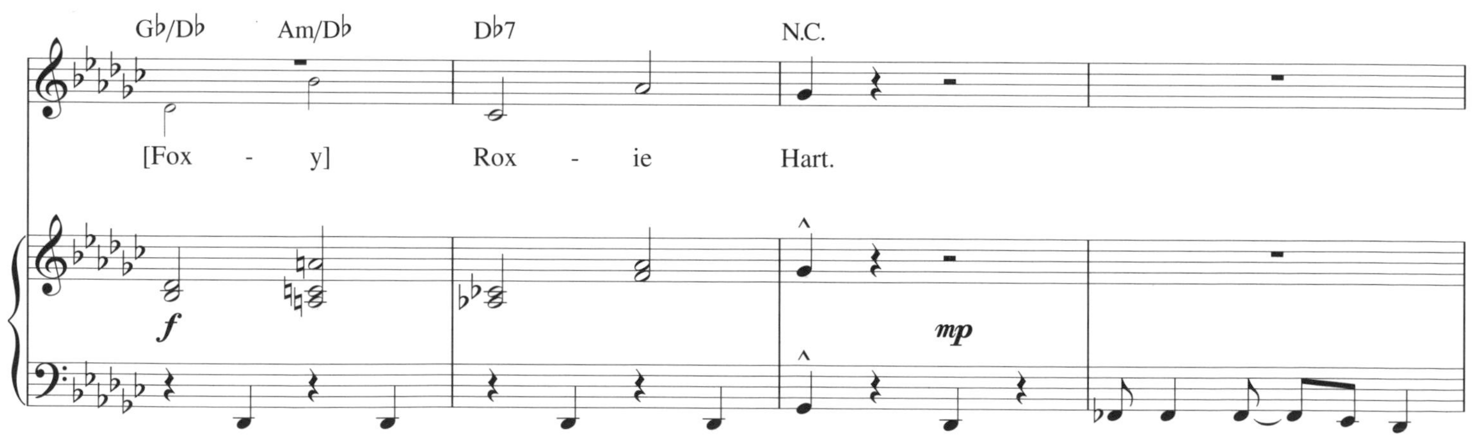
Gb/Db
Am/Db
Db7
N.C.
[Fox - y] Rox - ie Hart.
f
mp

A♭6
Adim7
They're gon - na wait out - side in line to get to see
mf
E♭7/B♭
E♭7
A♭6
Rox - ie, Think of those au - to - graphs I'll
sfz
Adim7
E♭7/B♭
E♭7
C7
sign: "Good luck to you, Rox - ie." And I'll ap - pear in a
Fm
C
Fm
lav - a - liere that goes all the way down to my waist.
sffz

D7
Gm
E♭7 D♭(add2)/F F♯m6 E♭7/G
Here a ring, there a ring, ev - 'ry - where a ring - a - ling, but al - ways in the
cresc.
Fdim/A♭ F♯dim/A E♭7/B5 E♭
N.C.
A♭
best of taste.
Spoken: I'm a star. And they love me, and I love them. And they love me for loving them and I love them for loving me. And we love each other. That's because none of us got enough love in our childhood. And that's showbiz, kid.
I'm giv - ing
repeat ad lib.
mf
Adim7
E♭7
up my hum - drum life, I'm gon - na be Rox - ie.
A♭7
D♭6
I made a scan - dal and a star.

D♭
E7♯11
And So - phie Tuck - er - 'll shit, I know, to
Fm(add4)
B♭6
A♭/E♭
A♭dim/E♭
D♭dim/E♭
E♭7
see her name get billed be - low
Fox - y Rox - ie
N.C.
Hart.
sfz
mf
gradually fade
p

HEAVEN HELP MY HEART

from *Chess*

Words and Music by BENNY ANDERSSON,
TIM RICE and BJORN ULVAEUS

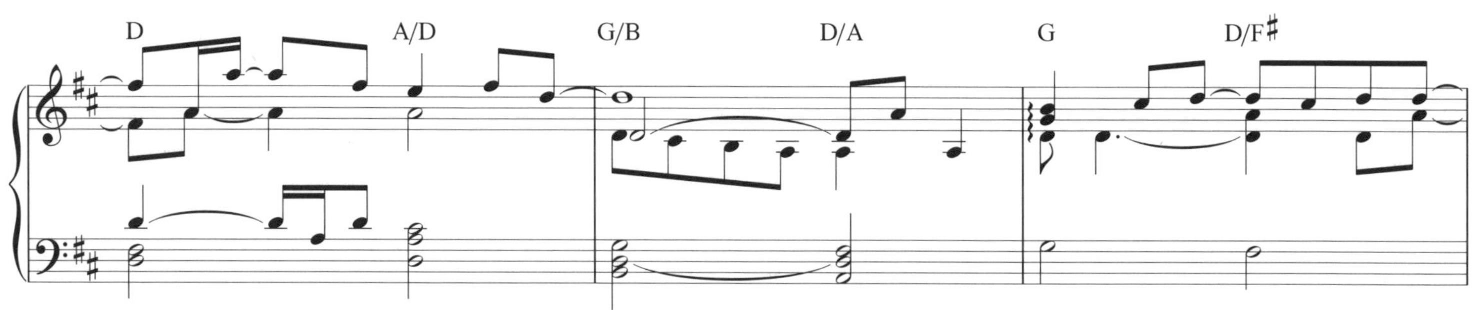

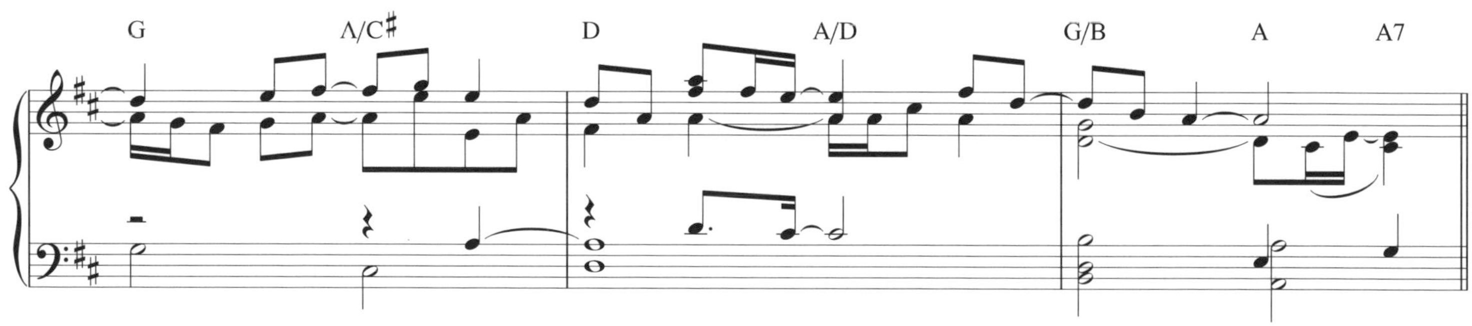

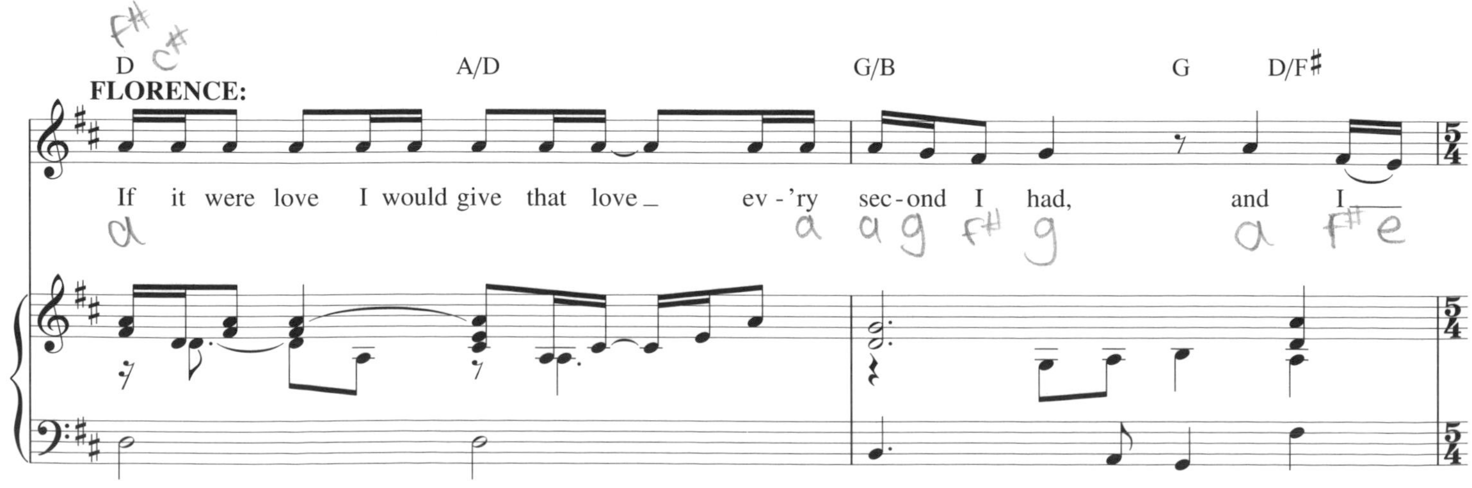

Em
A/C♯
A7
F♯m
Bm
F♯7/A♯
do. Did I know where he'd lead me to? Did I
Bm
Bm/A
E/G♯
E
A
(G/B)
A/C♯
(D)
plan do-ing all of this for the love of a man? Well, I let it
D
A/D
G/B
D/A
hap-pen an-y-how and what I'm feel-ing now
A/G
D/F♯
G/B
(Bm)
Em
has no eas-y ex-pla-na-tion. Rea-son plays no part,

Em
Em/D
A/C♯
A
D/F♯
D
A/C♯
heav - en, help my heart.
I
G/B
G
Gm
D/F♯
love him too much.
What if he saw my whole ex - is - tence
G
Em
A
turn - ing a - round a word, a smile,
a
D
D/F♯
G
A
D
A/D
touch?

G/B
Asus
A7
D
A/D
One of these days, and it won't be long, he'll know
G/B
G
D/F♯
Em
A/C♯
A7
more a - bout me than he should.
All my dreams will be un - der -
F♯m
Bm
F♯7/A♯
Bm
Bm/A
E/G♯
E
stood, no sur - prise, noth - ing more to learn from the
A
(G/B)
A/C♯
(D)
D
A/D
look in my eyes. Don't you know that time is not my friend, I'll

G/B D/A A/G D/F♯
fight it to the end, hop-ing to keep that best of mo - ments
G/B (Bm) Em Em Em/D A/C♯ A
when the pas - sions start. Heav - en, help my heart
D/F♯ D A/C♯ G/B G
the day that I find
Gm D/F♯ G Em
sud-den-ly I've run out of se-crets, sud-den-ly I'm not al - ways
3/4

A
D
D/F♯
G
D/F♯
on his mind.
G
D
molto rit.
G
a tempo
D/F♯
Em
May-be it's best to love a strang-er, well, that's what I've done— heav-en,
A6
A7
ten.
D
A/D
help my heart.
meno mosso
G/D
A7sus/D
rit.
D
Heav-en, help my heart.
rit.

THE MUSIC AND THE MIRROR

from *A Chorus Line*

Music by MARVIN HAMLISCH
Lyric by EDWARD KLEBAN

To have some - one to be.
Use me.
Choose me.
rall.
rall.
God, I'm a danc-er, a danc - er danc - es!
a tempo
Give me some-bod - y to dance with.
a tempo
Give me a place to fit in.
3
Help me re-turn to the world of the liv-ing by
3
3
show-ing me how to be - gin.
Moderate 4
a tempo
f

accel.
Play me the mu - sic. Give me the chance to come
accel.
through. All I ev - er need - ed was the mu -
- sic, and the mir - ror, and the chance to
dance for you.

Give me a job, and you in - stant - ly get me in - volved.
If you give me a job then the rest of the crap will get
solved.
Put me to work, you would think
that by now I'm al - lowed.
I'll

do
you
proud!
ff
Throw me a rope to grab on to.
Help me to prove that I'm
strong.
Give me the chance to look for - ward to say - in': "Hey,

lis - ten, they're play - in' my song."
Play me the
3
mu - sic.
Give me the chance to come through.
8va
loco
All I ev - er need - ed was the mu - sic, and the mir -
- ror, and the chance to

dance.
Play me the
pp cresc. poco a poco
mu - sic.
Play me the mu - sic.
Play me the
mu - sic.
Give me the chance to come through.
All I ev - er need-
8va
ffz

- ed was the mu - sic, and the mir - ror, and the chance
to dance.
for
you.
8vb

ANGELS, PUNKS AND RAGING QUEENS

from *Elegies for Angels, Punks and Raging Queens*

Words by BILL RUSSELL
Music by JANET HOOD

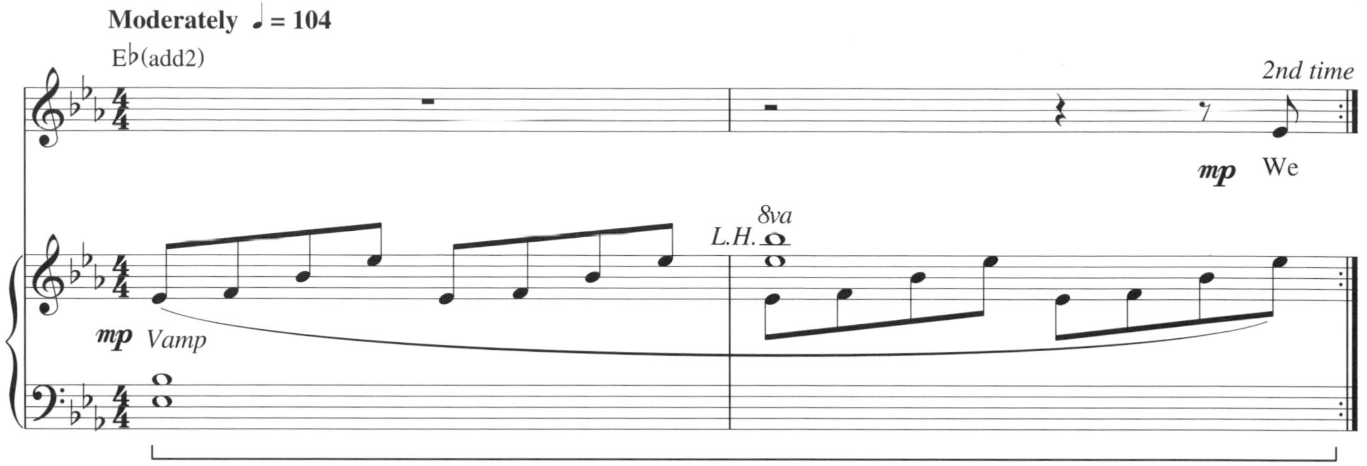

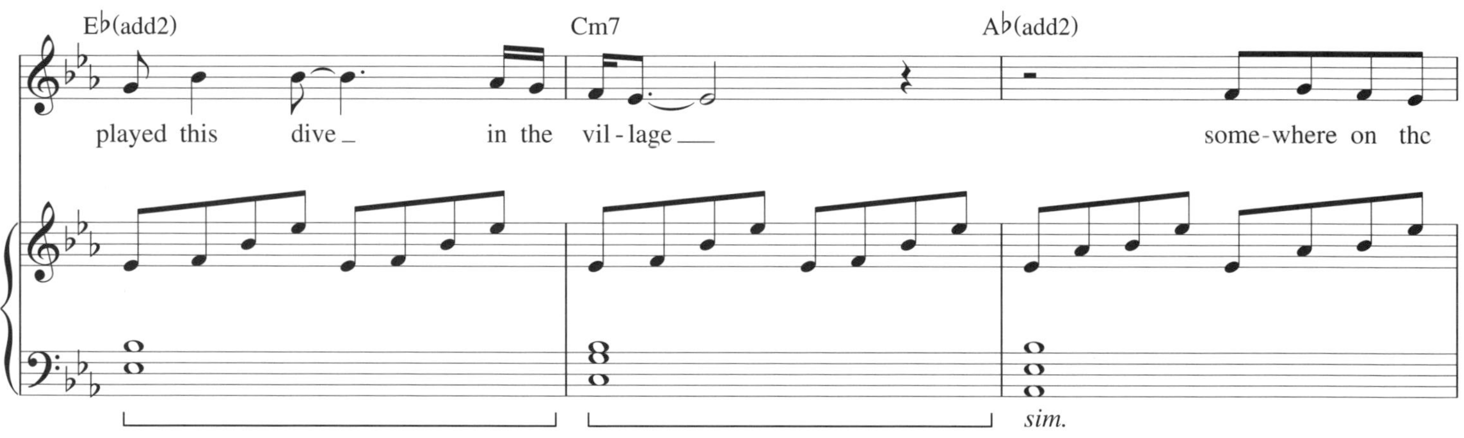

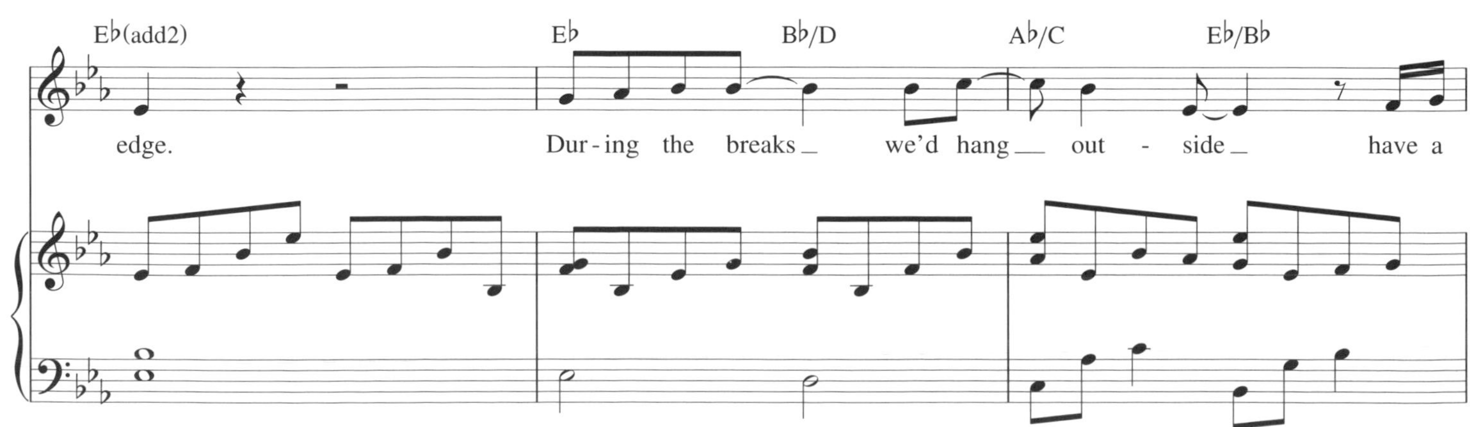

Db/Ab
Ab
Fm7(add11)
Fm
Eb
Db(add2)
smoke sit-tin' on a ledge.
I'd watch the pa-rade as it
Ab(add2)/C
Cb(add2)
Gb(add2)
Ab(add2)
passed by, the junk-ies and hot-to-trot teens.
And it
Abmaj9/Bb
Gm/Bb
Gb/Ab
Ab(add2)
Eb/G
Db/Ab
Ab
felt so right to be shar-ing the night with an-gels, punks and
F7sus4
F7
Bb7sus4
Eb(add2)
rag-ing queens.
We
L.H.
8va

Eb(add2)
Cm7
Ab(add2)
played that gig — for a long time. Got to know some

Eb(add2)
Eb
Bb/D
Ab/C
Eb/Bb
folks. Gave them some change, — or took — their cards, — heard their schemes, —

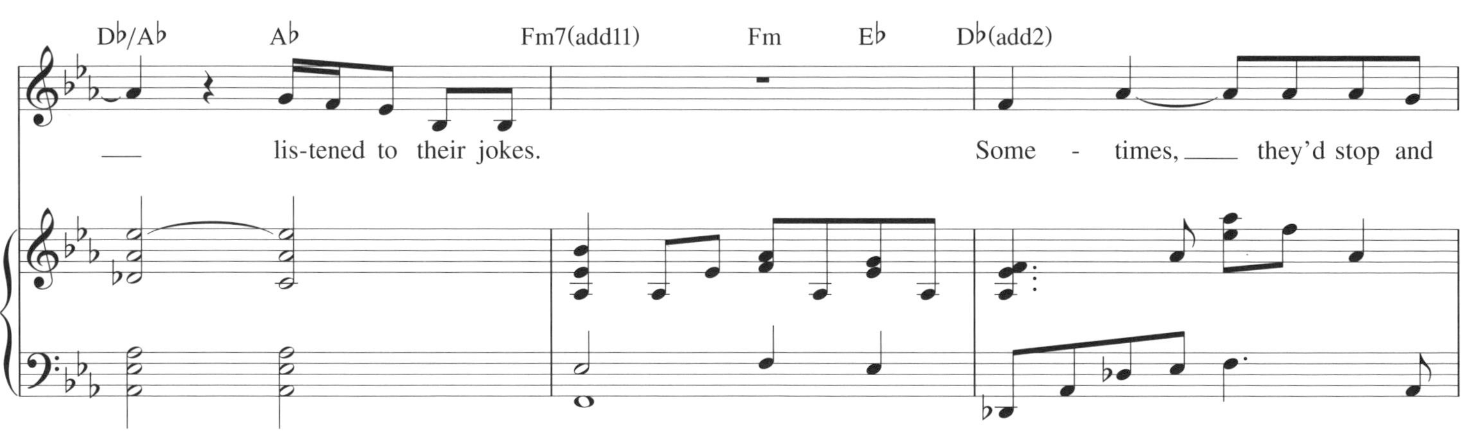
Db/Ab
Ab
Fm7(add11)
Fm
Eb
Db(add2)
— lis-tened to their jokes. Some - times, — they'd stop and

Ab(add2)/C
Cb(add2)
Gb(add2)
Ab(add2)
hear my song — en route to their fab - u - lous scenes. — And I

A♭maj9/B♭
Gm/B♭
G♭/A♭
A♭(add2)
E♭/G
D♭/A♭
A♭
still get laughs from old pho-to-graphs with an - gels, punks and
F7sus4
F7
B♭7sus4
E♭(add2)
rag - ing queens.
mf
Well I
rit.
Rubato
E♭m9
B♭m7
G♭(add2)
D♭(add2)/F
F+7
loved that time in the vil-lage
Though I still don't know what it
mf
G♭maj7
C♭9
D♭/A♭
F/A
B♭m7
G♭m6
means.
Ma-trons and whores in-tel-lec-tu-al bores

Db/F
Cb/Gb
Gb
Eb7sus4
Eb7
Ab7sus4
a tempo
Db(add2)
an - gels, punks and rag - ing queens.
Db(add2)
Bbm7
pp
I pass that place like a phan-tom.
rit.
a tempo
pp
Gb(add2)
Db(add2)
Db
Ab/C
Ev-'ry-thing has changed.
That lou-sy dive is a
Gb/Bb
Db/Ab
Cb/Gb
Gb
Ebm7(add11)
Ebm
Db
sleek bou - tique,
pri - or - i - ties re - ar - ranged. I

C♭(add2)
G♭(add2)/B♭
B♭♭(add2)
F♭(add2)
long for the mix of the bad old days, the ball gowns and torn up
mf
G♭(add2)
Rubato
G♭/A♭
Fm/A♭
F♭/G♭
E♭m/G♭
jeans.
f
And I sing this song for the souls who've gone; sweet
E♭m9
D♭(add2)/F
G♭(add2)
Gm7(♭5)
E♭m7/A♭
a tempo
D♭(add2)
an - gels, punks and rag - ing queens.
p
B♭m7
G♭(add2)
D♭
Oo
rit.

I'M STILL HERE

from *Follies*

Music and Lyrics by
STEPHEN SONDHEIM

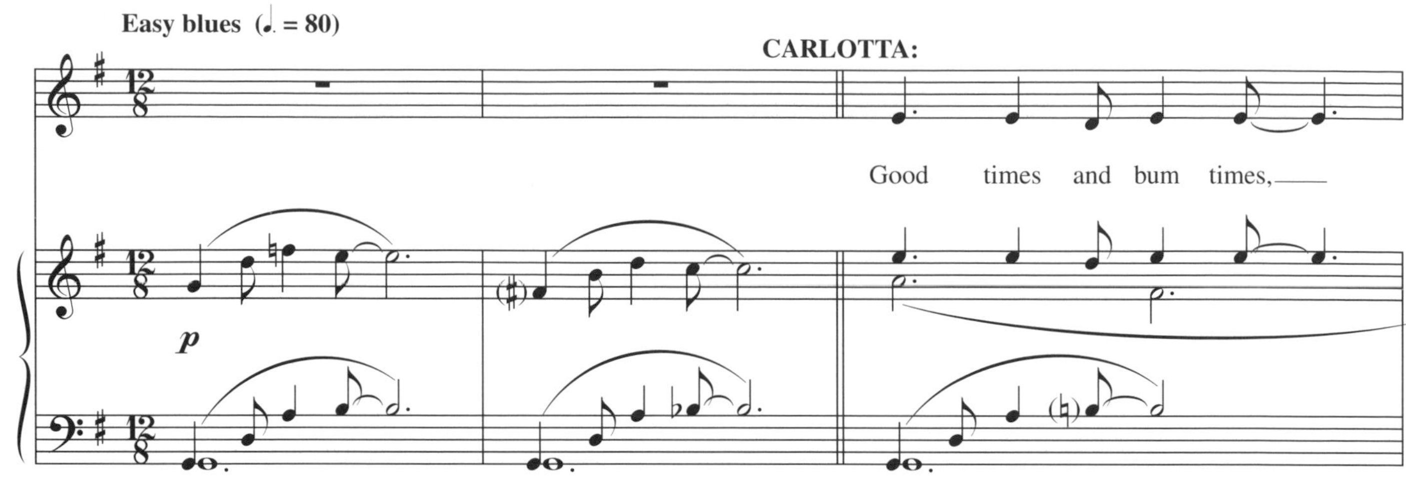

I've stuffed the dail - ies
In my shoes,
Strummed u - ke - le - les,
Sung the blues,
Seen all my dreams dis - ap - pear,
But I'm here.
I've slept in shan - ties,
Guest of the W. P. A.,
But I'm here.
mp sim.

Danced in my scan - ties,
Three bucks a night was the pay,

But I'm here.
I've stood in bread - lines
mf

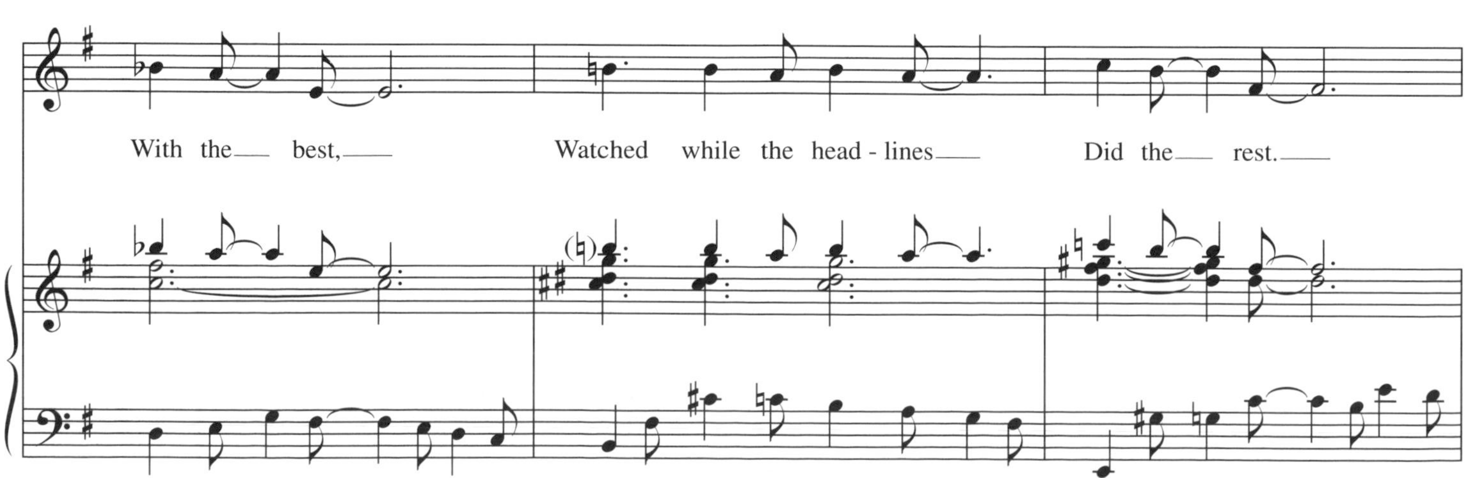
With the best,
Watched while the head - lines
Did the rest.

In the De - pres - sion was I de - pressed? No - where
dim.
near.
I met a big fi - nan - cier, And I'm
mp
here.
mf

I've been through Gand - hi,
Wind - sor and Wal - ly's af - fair,
And I'm here.
A - mos 'n' An - dy,
Mah - jongg and plat - i - num hair,
And I'm here.
I got through A - bie's
I - rish Rose,
Five Di - onne ba - bies,
Ma - jor Bowes,

Had hee - bie - jee - bies For Bee - be's Bath - y - sphere.
I lived through Bren - da Fra - zier And I'm
here. I've got - ten through
Her - bert and J. Ed - gar Hoo - ver,
f

Gee, that was fun and a half.
When you've been through
Her - bert and J. Ed - gar Hoo - ver,
An - y - thing else is a laugh.
I've been through Re - no,
mf
p
as before

I've been through Bev - er - ly Hills,
And I'm here.
Reef - ers and vin - o,
Rest cures, re - li - gion and pills,
But I'm here.
Been called a pink - o
Com - mie tool,
Got through it stink - o
poco cresc.
mp

By my pool.
I should have gone to an act - ing school, That seems
p
clear.
Still some - one said, "She's sin - cere,"
So I'm here.
mf
Black sa - ble one day,
Next day it goes in - to hock,

But I'm here.
Top bill - ing Mon - day,
Tues - day you're tour - ing in stock,
But I'm here.
First you're an - oth - er
Sloe - eyed vamp,
Then some - one's moth - er,
Then you're camp.
Then you ca - reer from ca - reer

to ca - reer.
I'm al - most through my mem - oirs, And I'm
here. I've got - ten through
"Hey, la - dy, are - n't you whoo - zis?
f

Wow! What a look - er you were."
Or, bet - ter yet,
"Sor - ry, I thought you were whoo - zis.
What - ev - er hap - pened to her?"
Good times and bum times, I've seen 'em all and, my dear, I'm still here.

Plush vel - vet some - times,
Some - times just pret - zels and beer,
But I'm here.
I've run the gam - ut,
A to Z.
Three cheers and dam - mit,
C'est la vie.
I got through all of last year,
And I'm here.

Lord knows, at least I've been there,
And I'm here!
Look who's here!
I'm still
here!

LIFE WITH HAROLD

from *The Full Monty*

Words and Music by
DAVID YAZBEK

Fmaj7
B♭9
C
catch I have caught. He would buy me the moon if the
A7
Dm7
G7
D♭7
moon could be bought. I'm tell - in' you: You got - ta love that
C6
man. I real - ly love
that man.
Dm7
G9
C6
He likes me dressed to the nines.

Dm7
G9
I say two words and then "Ta - da!"
There's me com-plete - ly in
C6
Fmaj7
Pra - da.
And I've got the boots that go with the
B♭9
C
A7
belt that goes with the bag that goes with my won - der - ful life with
Dm7
G7
D♭7
C6
Har - old.
You got - ta love that man.

Dm7
G9
(scat syllables)
mf
C6
Dm7
G9
C6
Fmaj7
B♭9
C
A7
Dm7
gliss.

G7
D♭7
C6
8va
f
ad lib. riff
God, I love that
man.
Dm7
G9
C6
But late - ly he's work - ing too hard.
I keep on tell - ing him how we
Dm7
G9
should take a few weeks in

C6
Fmaj7
Mau - ii. And we'll feel the breeze and samp - le the
B♭9
C
A7
poi and go see Don Ho and I'll say, "Oh boy, how I love you,
Dm7
G9
Em7
Har - old." I hit the jack - pot with Har - ry - y - y
A7
Fmaj7
B♭9
y! He's a gem, he's a beaut. He looks

C
A
Dm7
cute in a suit and he loves me to boot. I'm tell - ing you, —
G9
C
You got - ta love that man. Love that
man. I love that man.
I love that man.
Cmaj9

I WANT TO GO TO HOLLYWOOD

from the Broadway Musical *Grand Hotel*

Words and Music by
MAURY YESTON

A E+ Em/A E+ A E+ Em/A E+
I wan-na be that girl in the mir-ror there. I wan-na be that girl with gold - en hair.
A E+ Em/A E+ F#7 E(add2)/G# F#7
Up on a sil - ver screen, most ev - 'ry-where in the world.
B7(add4) E7sus E7 A(add2) B7#5 E9♭5
I want to go to Hol-ly - wood! Talk-ies! I mean the pic-tures.
A E+ Em/A E+ A E+ Em/A E+
I wan-na have a hot time ev - 'ry night, get out and raise a lit - tle Fahr - en-heit,

A E+ Em/A E+ F♯7 E(add2)/G♯ F♯7
knock ev - 'ry Duke and Count and Bar - on right off his feet!
B7(add4) E7sus E7 C♯7♯5 Em/F♯ F♯7
I'll be that girl that's un - der - stood! Oh!
B7(add4) E7sus E7 A9 G/B Cm A7/C♯ Cm G/B A9
I want to go to Hol - ly - wood. I wan - na sing the
D9 A9
blues. I wan - na wear nice shoes and drink il - le - gal
sim.

B7
G7
E9♯5
booze in ev - 'ry late-night spot for "Le Jazz Hot." _
A E+ Em/A E+ A E+ Em/A E+
I wan-na break-fast, lunch and din - ner there, if I'm a big box of - fice win - ner there.
A E+ Em/A E+ F♯7 E(add2)/G♯ F♯7
I'll be the most well - known Ber-lin - er there ev - er ___ was! ___
B7(add4) E7sus E7 A(add2) G♯+ Em/G F♯7 F♯7/A♯
I want to go to Hol-ly - wood, so

B7(add4)
E7sus
E7
Bb(b5)/A
I can get far a - way from:
Bb(b5)/A
Abm7b5
Fried - rich - stras - se. My cold wa - ter flat. The so - fa
that I sleep on be - hind the screen.
Bm7b5
The nois - y lodg - er in the
sim.
Abm7b5
next room. My brok - en hand mir - ror. My brok - en cof - fee pot.

Bm7♭5
B♭(♭5)/A
If things get brok - en, they stay brok - en in Fried - rich -
mf
A♭m7♭5
Bm7♭5
stras - se. The worn - out bris - tles on your hair - brush. The pen - nies
p subito
A♭m7♭5
need - ed for the heat ev - 'ry hour. And when you get sick, you
B♭(♭5)/A
D(add2)/E
stay sick in Fried - rich - stras - se. Where you live with lit - tle
f

A
E+
soap and with hard - ly an - y hope.
mp
Em/A
E+
I wan-na be that girl in the mir-ror there. I wan-na be that
girl with gold - en hair. Up on a sil - ver screen, most ev - 'ry-where in the world.
F♯7
E(add2)/G♯
B7(add4)
E7sus
E7
B7
I want to go to Hol ly, I want to go, I want

E7sus
E7
A(add2)
G♯+
Em/A
F♯7
F♯7/A♯
B7
__ to go, I want to go, I want _ to go, I want to go, I have to go, I have _
D/E
E9
A(add2)
G♯+
Em/G
F♯7
F♯7/A♯
B
B♭+/F♯
__ to go, I have to go, I have _ to go I have to go to Hol -
f
F♯m/B
B♭+/F♯
B
B♭+/F♯
F♯m/B
B♭+/F♯
B
B♭+/F♯
ly - wood, __ Hol -
F♯m/B
B♭+/F♯
G♯7
F♯(add2)/A♯
G♯m7♭5/B
G♯7/B♯
C♯9
ly - wood. __ I swear that girl in the

G♯m7♭5
C♯9
mir - ror,
girl in the mir - ror,
that girl in the
E/F♯
mir - ror
is go - ing to go
to
Hol -
rit.
B
B♭+/F♯
F♯m/B
ly - wood!
a tempo
accel.
B
gliss.
Ped.

THERE ARE WORSE THINGS I COULD DO

from *Grease*

Lyric and Music by WARREN CASEY
and JIM JACOBS

C
Cmaj7
F♯m7♭5
smile at them and bat my eyes,
B7
Em7
A7
press a - gainst them when we dance, make them think they stand a
Dmaj7
Bm7
E7
A7
chance, then re - fuse to see it through, that's a thing I'd nev - er
D7
Dm7
Gm7
do. I could stay home ev - 'ry night,
gliss.

C7
Fmaj7
B♭maj7
wait a-round for Mis - ter Right,
take cold show - ers ev - 'ry
Gm
A7
Dm
day and throw my life a - way for a dream that won't come true.
D7
Bm7
Em7
a tempo
Em7/D
I could hurt some - one like me
C
Cmaj7
F♯m7♭5
out of spite or jeal - ous - y,

B7
Emaj7
C♯m7
I don't steal and I don't lie but I can feel and I can
F♯m7♭5
B7
Em7
G/D
poco rit.
cry, a fact I'll bet you never knew.
poco rit.
Rubato
C
Am6
D7
But to cry in front of you, that's the worst thing I could
colla voce
N.C.
G
a tempo
C
rit.
Cm
Gmaj9
do.
a tempo
rit.

I CAN HEAR THE BELLS

from *Hairspray*

Music by MARC SHAIMAN
Lyrics by MARC SHAIMAN and SCOTT WITTMAN

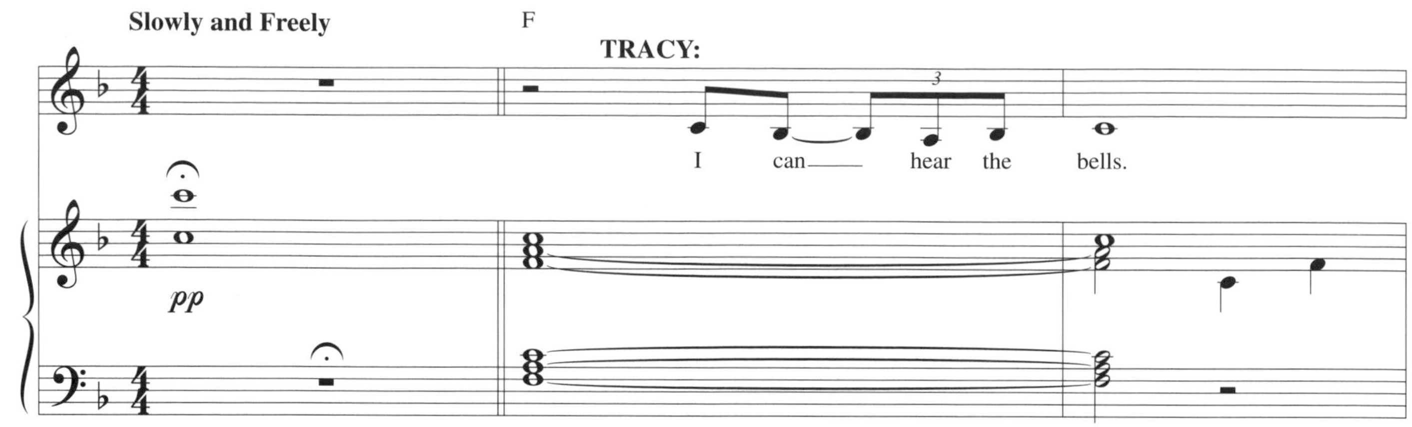

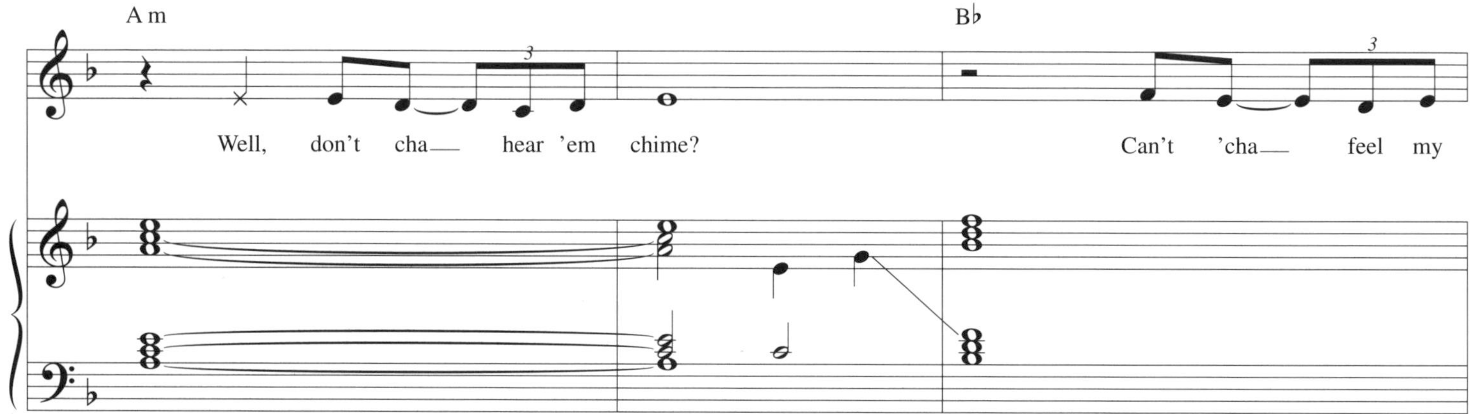

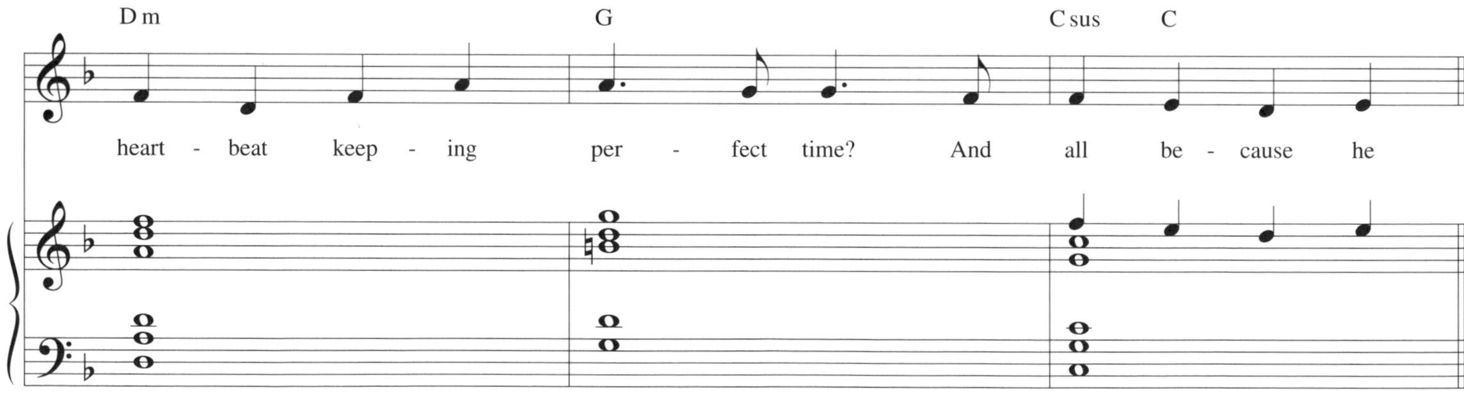

B♭
F/A
heart was un-pre-pared when he tapped me and knocked me off my feet.
G7sus
G7
B♭maj9/C
F
One lit-tle touch, now my life's com - plete. 'Cause when he nudged me, love
mp
D m
put me in a fix. Yes, it hit me just like a ton of bricks. Yes, my
B♭
F/A
F/G
G7
heart burst. Now I know what life's a-bout. One lit - tle touch and love's

F/C
C sus
C
F
F/E
knocked me out, and
I can hear the bells.
My head is spin - ning.
mf
D m
D m/C
B♭
I can hear the bells.
Some - thing's be - gin - ning.
Ev - 'ry - bod - y says that a
F/A
F/G
G 7
D m/C
C
B♭/C
C
girl who looks like me
can't win his love. Well, just
wait and see, 'cause
F
F/E
D m
I can hear the bells.
Just hear them chim - ing.
I can hear the bells. My
mf

Dm/C
B♭
F/A
temp - 'ra - ture's climb - ing. I can't con - tain my joy 'cause I fin - 'ly found the boy I've been
F/G
G7
C7sus
F
miss - in'. Lis - ten! I can hear the be - ells.
(ding!)
mp
B♭/C
F
D♭sus
D♭
G♭
G♭/F
E♭m
Round one, he'll ask me on a date, and then round two, I'll
f
mf

C♭
G♭/B♭
primp, but won't be late be - cause round three's when we kiss in - side his car. Won't
G♭/A♭
A♭7
G♭/D♭
D♭
D♭sus2
D♭
G♭
go all the way, but I'll go pret - ty far. Then round four, he'll
mf
G♭/F
E♭m
ask me for my hand, and then round five, we'll book the wed - ding band, so by
C♭
G♭/B♭
G♭/A♭
A♭7
round six, Am - ber, much to your sur - prise, this heav - y - weight cham - pi - on

E♭m/D♭ D♭ C♭/D♭ D♭
G♭
G♭/F
takes the prize and I can hear the bells. My ears are ring - ing.
E♭m
E♭m/D♭ C♭
I can hear the bells. The brides-maids are sing - ing. Ev - 'ry - bod-y says that a
G♭/B♭
A♭7sus A♭7
E♭m/D♭ D♭ C♭/D♭ D♭
guy who's such a gem won't look my way. Well, the laugh's on them 'cause
G♭
G♭/F E♭m
I can hear the bells. My fa - ther will smile… I can hear the bells. …as he

E♭m/D♭ C♭ G♭/B♭

walks me down the aisle. My moth-er starts to cry, but I can't see 'cause Link and I are French-

G♭/A♭ A♭7 D♭7sus G♭

kiss - in'. Lis - ten! I can hear the bells.

(ding!)

C♭/G♭ G♭ D sus D

G G/F♯ Em

I can hear the bells. My head is reel - in'. I can hear the bells. I

* Optional ending

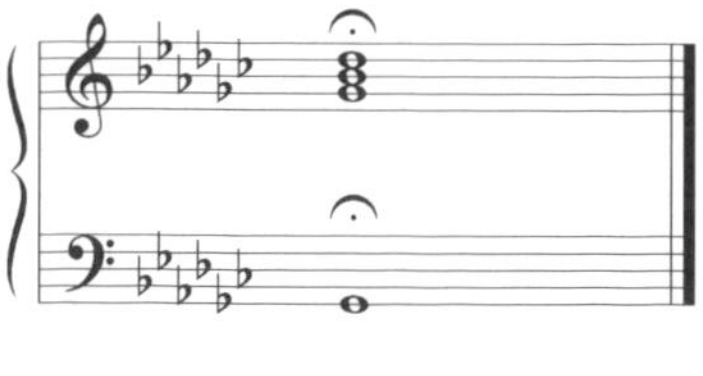

Em/D
C
G/B
can't stop the peal - in'.
Ev - 'ry - bod - y warns that he won't like what he'll see, but
f
G/A
A7
Em/D D C/D D
G
I know that he'll look in - side of me. Yeah, I can hear the bells. To -
ff
G/F♯
Em
Em/D
day's just the start 'cause I can hear the bells, and 'til death do us part. And
C
G/B
Am7
e - ven when we die we'll look down from up a - bove, re - mem - ber - ing the night that we
mp

G/B
G7/B
C
two fell in love. We both will share a tear, and he'll
G/A
A
D7sus
whis - per as we're rem - i - ni - scin'. Lis - ten! I can hear the
colla voce
(ding!)
G
G7/F
Em7
bells. I can hear the bells.
rit.
Cm/E♭
G
I can hear the bells.

MISS BALTIMORE CRABS
from *Hairspray*

Music by MARC SHAIMAN
Lyrics by MARC SHAIMAN
and SCOTT WITTMAN

Fm
Fm6
Fm(maj7)
Fm
D♭9♯11
D♭9
Child - hood dreams for me were cracked when that damn Shir - ley Tem - ple stole
D♭9♯11
D♭9
Gm7♭5
C7sus
C7♭9
B7
C7
my frick - in' act. But the crown's in the vault from when I won "Miss Bal - ti - more
Fm
F7
B♭m7
D♭6/E♭
E♭9♯5
Crabs." Those poor run-ner-ups might still hold some grudg-es They
Cm7
F9
pad - ded their cups, but I screwed the judg - es. Those broads thought they'd win if a

Db9 G7b9/D G7/D Db9 C7 G7b5/Db C7b9 C9 C7b9
plate they would spin in their dance. Not a chance! 'Cause I
Fm Fm6 Fm(maj7) Fm Db9#11 Db9
hit the stage, ba - tons a - blaze, while belt - ing high 'C's and pre -
Db9#11 Db9 Gm7b5 C7sus C7b9
par - ing souf - flés! But that trip - le som - er - sault was how I clinched "Miss Bal - ti - more
Fm F7 Bbm7 Bbm7/Eb Ddim/Eb
Crabs!" A ty-coon I wed, so cud-dly and fun-ny The

Cm7
F9
A♭9/D
A♭9
old fart dropped dead, but left tons of mon - ey. So I bought this sta - tion so
G7
D♭7
C♭maj7/G
Fm7♭5/G
C+/G
D♭9
C7
all of the na - tion could see Ba - by
D♭7
E♭7
A♭m
A♭m6
A♭m(maj7)
A♭m
E9(♯11)
E9
Am-ber and me! And so, my dear, so short and stout, you'll nev-er be "in." So we're
E9♯11
E9
B♭m7♭5
E♭7♭9
kick - ing you out! You can't get past me kid. But it is - n't your fault. It's

Db♭m/E♭
Bdim7/E♭
E♭7
hard to get rid of "Miss Bal - ti - more
A♭m6
D♭m6
E♭7
Crabs"!
You can
bow and ex - alt, 'cause I was "Miss Bal - ti - more
A♭m
Crabs!"
A♭m6
Crabs! Crabs! Crabs!!!

I DON'T KNOW HOW TO LOVE HIM

from *Jesus Christ Superstar*

Words by TIM RICE
Music by ANDREW LLOYD WEBBER

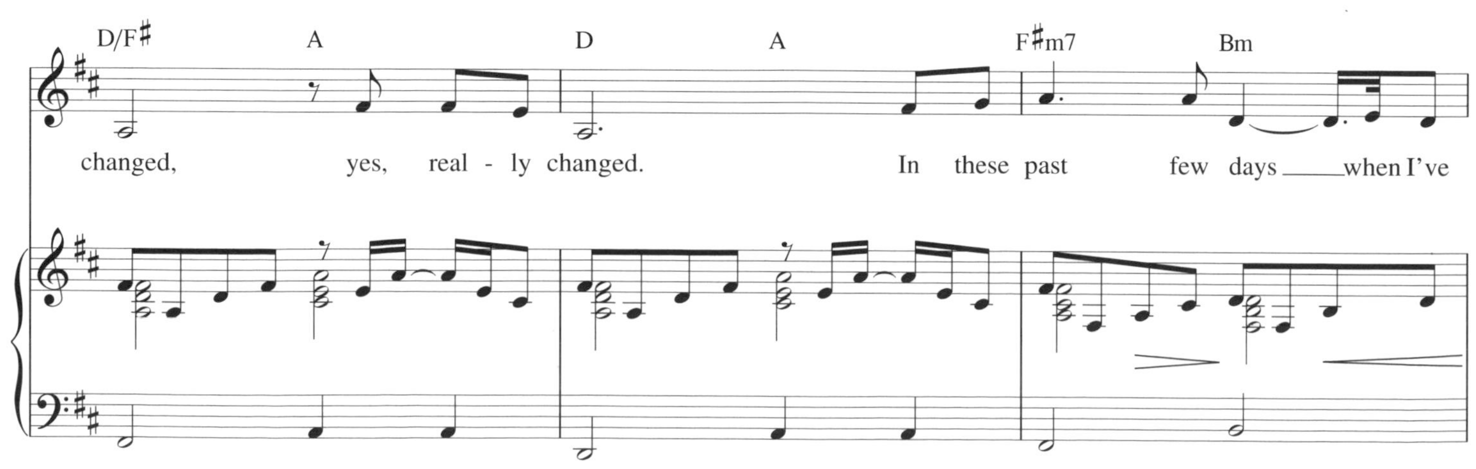

F♯m Bm G D/F♯ Em D Asus(add9) A
seen my-self I seem like some - one else
D G D G D G
I don't know how to take this I don't see why he
D/A A D A D A
moves me. He's a man, he's just a man, and I've
F♯m Bm F♯m Bm G D/F♯ Em D
had so man y men be fore in ver y man - y

Asus(add9)
A G D/F♯ Em7
D
ways. He's just one more.
G
F♯7
Bm Bm/A
Should I bring him down should I scream and shout? Should I speak of love,
cresc. poco a poco
G
D/A
C
G
D
let my feel-ings out? I nev - er thought I'd come to this.
f dim. poco a poco
G
D/F♯
Em
Asus(add9)
A
What's it all a - bout?

D
G
D
G
D
Don't you think it's rath - er fun - ny
G
D/A
A
I should be in this po - si - tion? I'm the
D/F♯
A
D
A
F♯m
Bm
one who's al-ways been So calm and cool
F♯m
Bm
G
D/F♯
Em7
D
no lov - er's fool run - ning ev - 'ry

Asus
A G D/F♯ Em7
D
G
F♯m7
show. He scares me so.
mf
cresc. poco a poco
Bm
Bm/A
G
D/A
C
G
D
G
D/F♯
I nev - er thought I'd come to this. What's it all a -
f
ff
f dim. poco a poco
Em
Asus(add9)
D
G D
bout? Yet if he said he

G D G D/A A
loved me, I'd be lost I'd be fright - ened. I could - n't
D/F♯ A D A F♯m Bm
cope, just could-n't cope. I'd turn my head,
F♯m Bm7 G F♯m Em D Asus A G D/F♯ Em7
I'd back a - way, I would - n't want to know. He scares me
D G D/F♯ Em7 D G D/F♯ Em7 D
so. I want him so. I love him so.
rall.
pp

I WILL BE LOVED TONIGHT

from *I Love You, You're Perfect, Now Change*

Lyrics by JOE DiPIETRO
Music by JIMMY ROBERTS

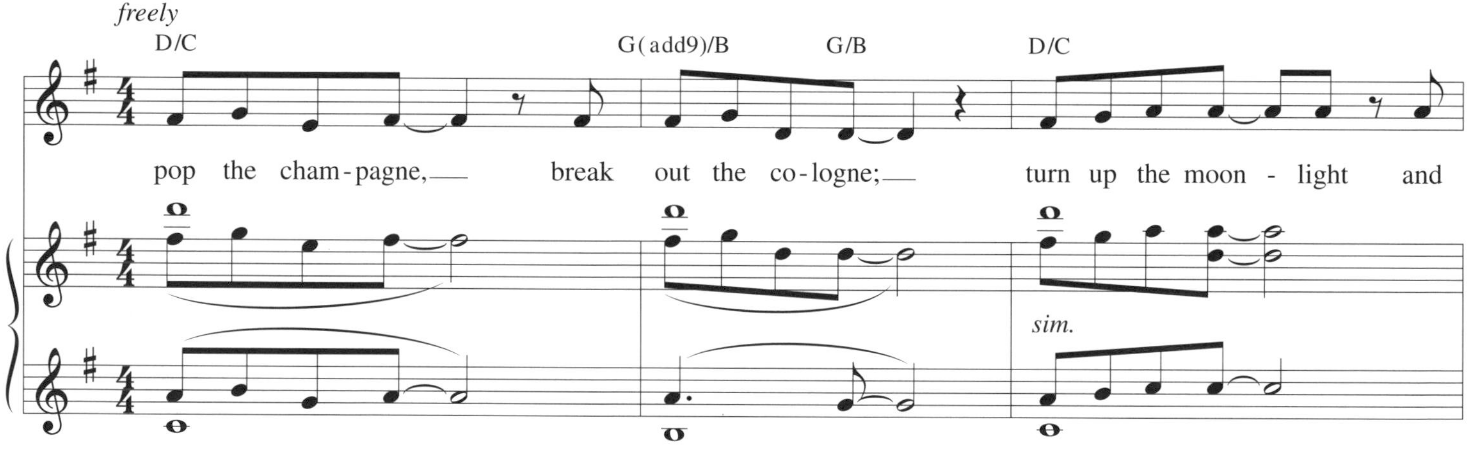

With a gentle beat ♩ = 96
C/E D/F♯ G D7sus/A D7/F♯ D7 G Gmaj7(no3)
I will be loved to - night. To
D/C Gmaj9/B G/B D/C
fon - dle his skin, to sav - or his lips; to nuz - zle his chin, to
G(add9)/B G/B G/F freely C(add9)/E G/D
move with his hips. Our words will be soft as we soft - ly ig - nite; and
a tempo A little faster
C/E D/F♯ G D7sus/A D7/F♯ D7 G Gmaj7(no3)
I will be loved to - night. You can
poco accel.

Moderately, with a beat ♩ = 112
D D/C G(add9)/B G/B C D D/C G(add9)/B G/B
go from week to week, you can go from year to year; not a
mf
Bb Bb(add9) C/Bb F(add9)/A F/A Fmaj9
hand placed on your cheek, not a whis - per in your
mp
C(add9) D D/C G(add9)/B G/B C
ear. You can make it through o - kay, you can
mf
D D/C G(add9)/B G/B Bb Bb(add9) C/Bb F(add9)/A F/A
live and laugh, and flirt. It's quite eas - y in the day;

slowing down
Em
freely
Em7
A7
Tempo I
D/C
G(add9)/B
G/B
it's just the nights that al-ways hurt. So
mp
rit.
rit.
D/C
G(add9)/B
G/B
D/C
let dark-ness come, 'cause that will be fine; for I'll have a soul en-
mp a tempo
mf
Bm7
G/B
G/F
freely
C(add9)/E
G/B
ten.
tan-gled in mine. We'll do as we please, and please... hold me tight. For
mp
a tempo
C/E
D/F♯
G
D7sus/A
D7/F♯
G
I will be loved,
poco a poco crescendo

C/E
D/F♯
E7/G♯
E7sus/A
Am
G/B
C
D/C
I will be loved.
Yes, I
Bm7
G/B
A9/C♯
will be loved
poco a poco cresc. e accel.
sub. mp
Am/D
D
Em/D
Am7/D
D7
Gently, In Tempo
G/F
to - night.
slower
rit.
mp
C(add9)/E
C/E
D/C
G(add9)
poco rit.
p
8va

STILL HURTING

from *The Last Five Years*

Music and Lyrics by
JASON ROBERT BROWN

C
F/A
B♭2
C
F/A
B♭2
Ja-mie ar-rived at the end of the line.
Ja-mie's con-vinced that the prob-lems are
mp flowing
C
Dmin7
C/E
D7/F♯
E7/G♯
mine.
Ja-mie is prob-a-bly feel-ing just fine,
And
F2/A
B♭2
G7/B
Csus
C
Dmin11
C2/E
F6/9
Csus
C
C/B
I'm still hurt - ing.
sub. p
mp
Amin9
F2
Amin9
What a-bout lies, Ja - mie? What a-bout things That you swore to be true?
mf legato

D9/F♯
F2
C/E
Dmin11
G(add 11)
What a-bout you, Ja-mie? What a-bout you?
C
F/A
B♭2
C
Ja - mie is sure some - thing won - der - ful died.
C
F/A
B♭2
C
Ja - mie de - cides it's his right to de - cide.
Dmin7
C/E
D7/F♯
E7/G♯
Ja - mie's got se - crets he does - n't con - fide, And

F2/A B♭2 G7/B Csus
I'm still hurt - ing.
(sempre mf)
molto cresc.
E♭/C D/C D♭/C C G/B
Go and hide and run a - way! Run a-way,
f
Amin7 D9 F6/9
run and find some - thing bet-ter!
mf
D♭/E♭ F/E♭ E/E♭ E♭
Go and ride the sun a - way! Run a-way,
f

Cmin7
A♭2
Fmin11
like it's sim-ple, Like it's right...
mf
mp
C
F/A
B♭2
C
F/A
B♭2
3
C
Dmin7
C/E
D/F♯
E7/G♯
F/A
B♭
G7/B
Csus
5
mf
Amin9
F2
Give me a day, Ja - mie! Bring back the lies, Hang them
8va

Amin9
D9/F♯
F2
C/E
back on the wall! May-be I'd see How you could be So cer-tain that
mp
Cmin7/E♭
D♭Maj11
G(add 11)
we Had no chance at all.
C
F/A
B♭2
C
F/A
B♭2
Ja-mie is o - ver and where can I turn? Cov-ered with scars I did no-thing to earn?
pp
C
Dmin7
C/E
D7/F♯
E7/G♯
May-be there's some-where a les-son to learn, But

F2/A
Gsus/B
F2/A
that would-n't change the fact,
That would-n't speed the time,
mf
Gsus/B
F2/A
Emin7
Once the foun - da - tion's cracked
And
F2
G(add 11)
I'm
Still
mf
colla voce
C
F/A
B♭2
C
rit.
F/A
B♭2
C
hurt - ing.
mp

SEE I'M SMILING

from *The Last Five Years*

Music and Lyrics by
JASON ROBERT BROWN

I stole this sweat-er from the cos - tume shop –
It makes me look like Dai-sy Mae.
See, we're laugh - ing —
I think we're gon-na be o -
kay.
I mean, we'll have to
try a lit tle har der
And bend things to and fro
To make

this love as spe-cial As it was five years a-go.
I mean, you made it to O-hi-o! Who knows
where else we can go?
I think you're real-ly gon-na like this show.
I'm pret-ty sure it does-n't suck.

See, you're laugh - ing, and I'm smil - ing, By a
riv - er in O - hi - o And you're mine...
We're do-ing fine.
p
sub. mf
I think we both can

see what could be bet-ter — I'll own when I was wrong.. With all
we've had to go through, We'll end up twice as strong. And so we'll
start a-gain this week-end, And just keep
roll-ing a-long...

I did-n't know you had to go so soon.
I thought we had a lit-tle time...
Look, what - e - ver, if you have to, Then you have to, so what - e - ver.
It's all right
We'll have to-night.
sub. f

You know what makes me cra-zy? I'm sor-ry, can I say this? You know what makes me nuts? The fact that we could
mf
be to-geth-er, Here to-geth-er, Shar-ing our night, spend-ing our time, And you are gon-na
choose some-one else to be with — no, you are. Yes, Ja-mie, that's ex-act-ly what you're do-ing: You could
be here with me, Or be there with them — As u-su-al, guess which you pick! No, Ja-mie, you do

not have to go to a-no-ther par - ty— with the same twen-ty jerks you al-read-y know. You could
stay with your wife on her fuck-ing birth - day; And you could, God for-bid, e-ven see my show! And I
know in your soul it must drive you cra - zy That you won't get to play with your lit-tle girl - friends—No, I'm
not —no, I'm not!—and the point is, Ja - mie, That you can't spend a sin-gle day That's not a-bout

You and you and no-thing but you. "Mah-ve-lous" no-vel-ist, you! Is-n't he
won-der-ful? Just twen-ty-eight! The sav-ior of writ-ing! You,
and you, and no-thing but you — Mi-les and pi-les of you, Push-ing through
win-dows and burst-ing through walls En route to the sky!
And I...
fff

I swear to God_ I'll nev-er un - der - stand_
How you can stand there,_ straight and
tall,
And see I'm cry - ing_
And not do a-ny-thing_ at all..._

SHADOWLAND

Disney Presents *The Lion King: The Broadway Musical*

Music by LEBO M and HANS ZIMMER
Lyrics by MARK MANCINA and LEBO M

This version has been adapted as a solo.

F
fall - en.
This shad - owed
Am
land,
this was our
Gsus
G
home.
The riv - er's
3
Am
Am/G
dry,
the ground has

F
bro - ken.
So I must
C
go,
now I must
E7sus
go.
E7
And where the
Am
jour - ney may lead me, let your prayers be my
F
F/G
mf

*optional cut to **

Dm
B♭maj7
C7
Dm
A7
**
D7(no 3rd)
cresc.
D2
Bm7♭5

E7sus
E7
Am
And where the jour - ney may
F
F/G
Am
lead you, let this prayer be your guide. Though it may
E7
take you so far - a - way, al - ways re - mem - ber your
Am
pride. And where the jour - ney may

F
F/G
Am
lead you, let this prayer be your guide. Though it may
take you so far-a-way, al-ways re-mem - ber your
E7
Am
pride. (ad lib.) Mm. Gi -
3
p
gi-za bu-ya-bo. Be - si-bo, my peo-ple, be-si-bo.
Am9

WHATEVER HAPPENED TO MY PART?

from *Monty Python's Spamalot*

Lyrics by ERIC IDLE
Music by JOHN DU PREZ and ERIC IDLE

Power Ballad (Mid-1970's Streisand)

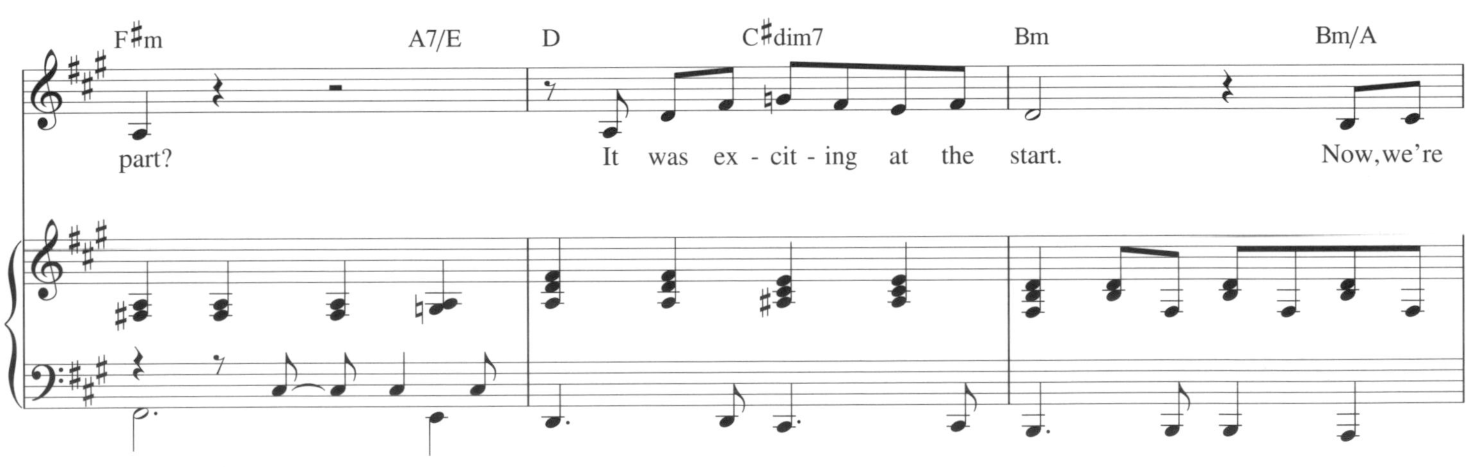

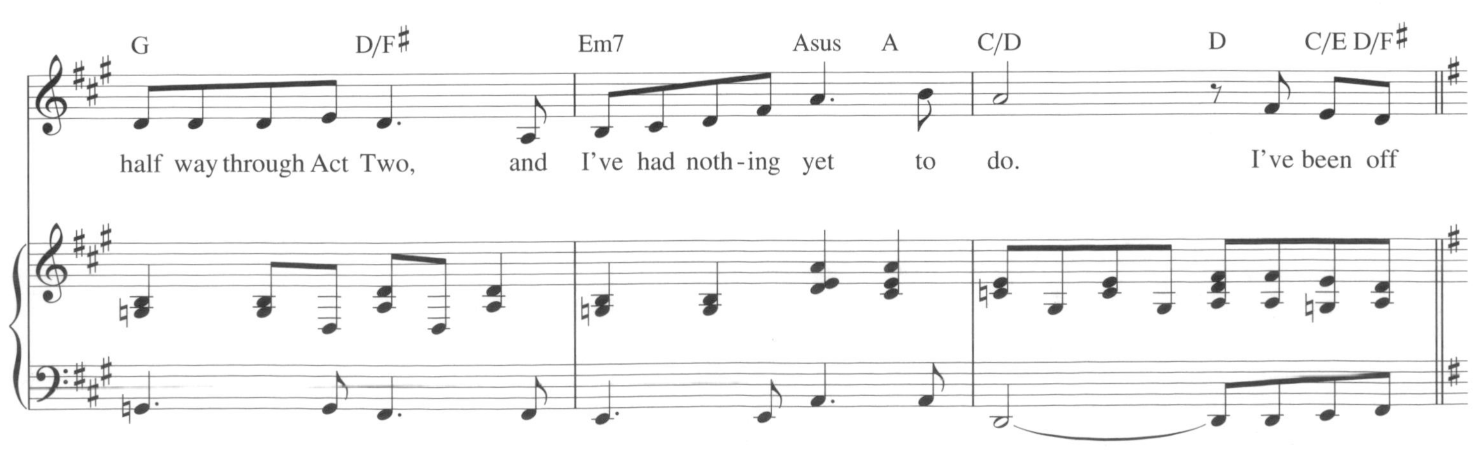

G A/G D(add2)/F♯ D/F♯ F(add2) G/F
stage for far too long. It's ag - es since I had a
C(add2)/E C/E Em7 A7
song. This is one un - hap - py di - va. The pro -
Em7 A Em Em7/D
duc - ers have de - ceived_ her. There is noth - ing I can sing from my
A/C♯ A A/C♯ C D6 D7 G/D D G
heart. What-ev - er hap-pened to my part? I am

Em7
D/F♯
sick of my ca - reer al-ways stuck in sec - ond gear, up to
detached
G Asus A D(add2)
C♯m7 F♯7sus F♯/A♯
here with frus-tra-tion and with fears. I've no Gram-my, no re-wards. I've no
Bm Bm/A Em7 Asus A
To - ny A-wards. I'm con-stant - ly re-placed by Brit-ney Spears. Brit-ney
p
cresc.
B♭m7/E♭ E♭7 A♭ Gm7♭5 C7
Spears! What-ev - er hap-pened to my
cresc.
rall.
mf a tempo

Fm
Ab7/Eb
Db
Cm7b5
F7/A
Bbm
Bbm/Ab
show? I was a hit. Now, I don't know. I'm with a
mp
Gb
Db/F
Ebm7
Absus
Ab
B/Db
Db
bunch of Brit-ish knights, pran-cing'round in wool - y tights! I might as
cresc.
F#
G#/F#
C#(add2)/F
C#/F
E(add2)
F#/E
well go to the pub. They've been out search - ing for a
f
B(add2)/D#
B/D#
D#m7
G#
D#m6
G#
shrub. Out shop-ping for a bush! Well, they can kiss my tush! It

D♯m
D♯m/C♯
G♯/B♯
G♯
seems to me they've real - ly lost the plot.
cresc.
B
C♯
What-ev - er hap-pened to my—
I'll call my a - gent, dam - mit—
what-ev - er hap-pened to my...
ff
molto rit.
Freely
N.C.
not yours... not yours... but my
Broadly
F♯
part?
B/F♯
C♯/F♯
F♯
molto rit.

WHEN YOU GOT IT, FLAUNT IT

from *The Producers*

Words and Music by
MEL BROOKS

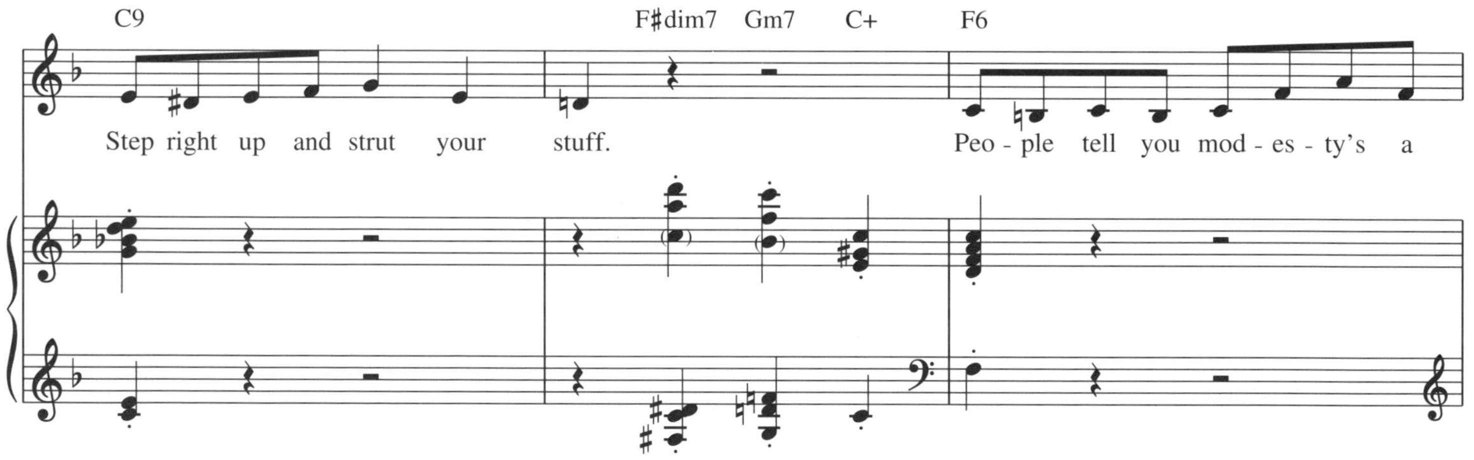

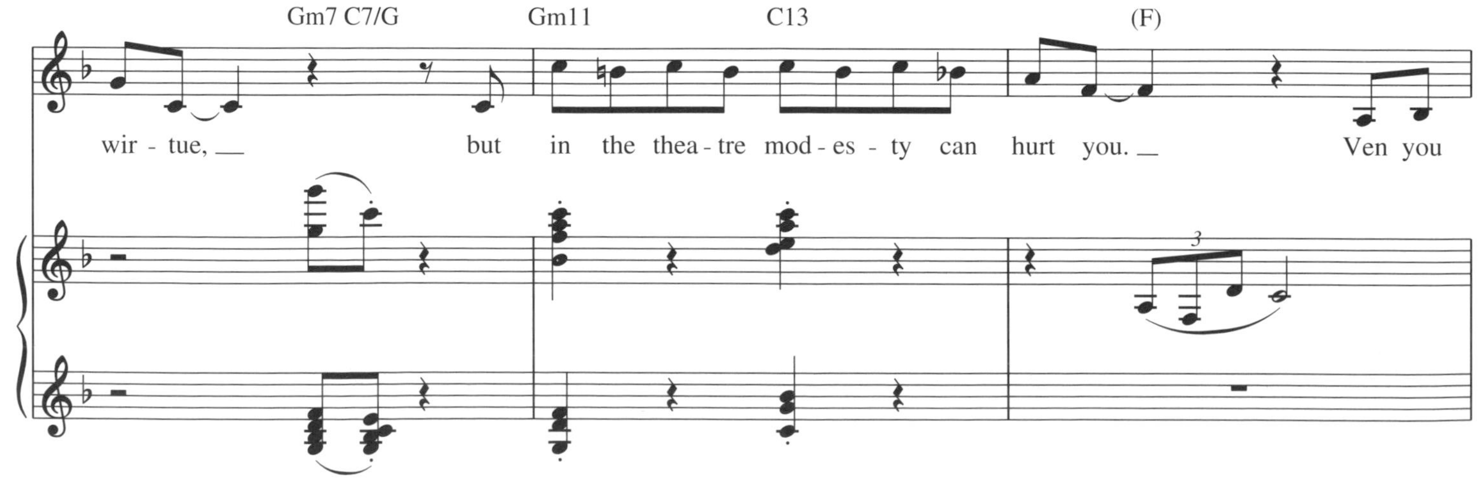

Ulla sings this song with a Swedish accent in the show.

F6/C
G9/D
C7
got it, flaunt it. Show your as - sets let 'em know you're
mp
Em7 A7
D9
G13
proud. Your good - ies you must push, stick your chest out, shake your tush, ven you
F6/C G9/C C7♭9 F6 Gm7/C
Cool Swing
F
got it, shout _ it out loud! _____ Ven you got it
mf
mp
G
C7
F6 F♯dim7 C13
show it put your hid - den trea - sures on dis - play

F6/9 Gm7 C9 Gm9 C11
Vi - o - lin - ists love to play an E - string But au - di - enc - es real - ly love a
F/A G#dim7 Gm7 C13 F6 G7
G - string Ven you got it, shout it.
mf
C7 A7 D7
Let the whole vorld hear vat you're a - bout Clothes may make the man, all a
G7 Gm9 Db7#5 C13 F6
girl needs is a tan ven you got it let it hang out. Ven

Sweetly
Em7♭5 A7 Dm A7♭9/D Dm Em7♭5 A7
straight 8ths
I was yust a lit - tle girl in Sve - den my thought-ful mo-ther gave me this ad -
mp
Dm Dm7 G7 C6 Am7
vice: If na-ture bles-ses you from top to bot - tom,
8va
6
Swing!
Dm11 G13 C13
show that top to bot-tom, don't think twice. Don't think
mf
Ab♭m9/D♭ D♭13 A♭m/D♭ B♭m/C♭ C♭/B♭ D♭/A♭
twice. Ven you
f

Broad swing
G6 G6/F♯ Em7 G6/D
A13 A13/G A13/F♯ A13/E
got it
share it.
ff
D7 D9
G6 E7/G♯ Am7 D9
Let the pub - lic feast up - on your charms.
G G/F♯ Em7 G/D
Am11 D7
Am11 D13
Peo - ple say that be - ing prim is prop - er,
But ev - 'ry show - girl knows that "prim" will
mf
G E♭9
A♭ A♭/G Fm9 A♭/E♭
stop her.
Ven you
got it,
f

Bb7
Eb7
Bbm/Db
give it.
Don't be self - ish, give it all a -
C7
Bbadd9/D
Ebdim7
C7/E
vay!
Don't be
F7
shy, be bold and cute,
show the
p
ff
Bb9b5
boys that birth - day suit
ven you
p
ff

"Going home"
Bbm9
Dbm7
got it
If you got it
f
Ab6/Eb
Bb9/Eb
Eb13
Once you got it
shout out hoo -
gliss.
Samba-straight 8ths
Eb7
Ab
ray!
ff
Ab/Gb
Db/F
Dbm/Fb
Eb7sus
fff

JUST ONE STEP

from *Songs for a New World*

Music and Lyrics by
JASON ROBERT BROWN

Moderately, but with an edge

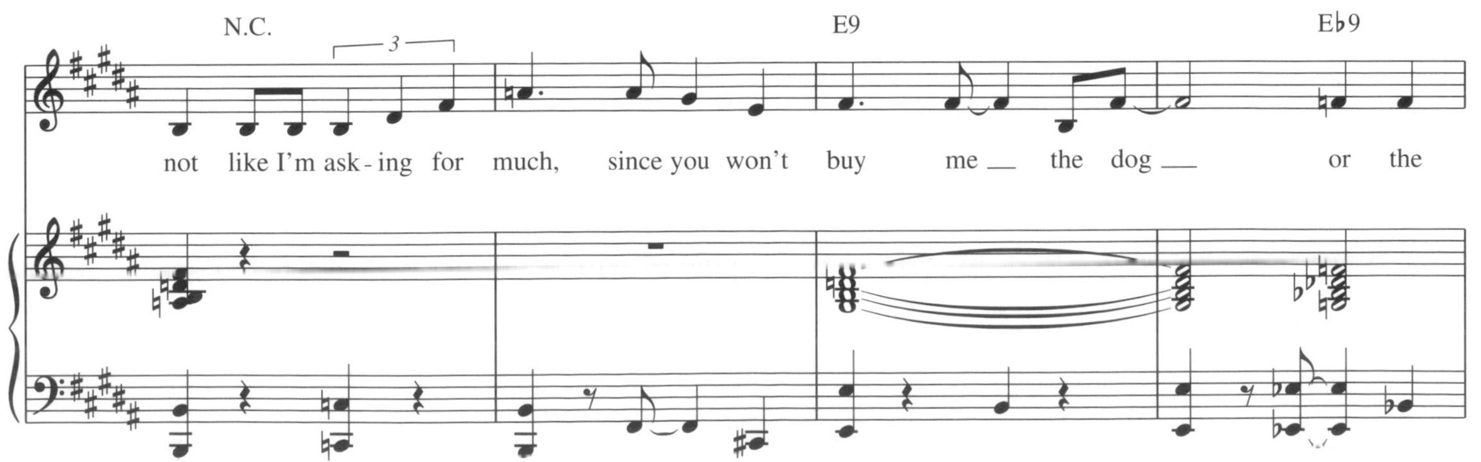

D9
D♭9
C9
beach house _ in Quogue (as if you did - n't have the mon - ey...).
B9
What else is new? _
B7 N.C.
3
I'm not gon-na fight for a coat, so nev - er mind, Mur-ray.
B7
3
E9
If that's what's im-por-tant to you, at least I know where _ I

E♭9
D9
D♭9
C9
stand, so Mur-ray, strike up the band! 'Cause the time has come for ac-tion.
F+
Here's what I'll do:
D6/E
E(add2)
D6/E
E5
Clear - ly I'm not want - ed an - y - more,
D6/E
E(add2)
Bm7/E
E7
D6/E
E(add2)
now I'm not so young and beau - ti - ful. That's o - kay.

D6/E
E5
F#
G/F#
I've faced de - feat be - fore. I'm not gon-na kvetch and I'm
Ab/F#
A/F#
Bb/F#
B/F#
C/F#
C#/F#
E7
not gon-na cry. It's not gon-na get me what I want-ed so I'm sim-ply gon-na take one step,
mf
8vb
Eb9/E
D9/E
E7
one ti - ny step, and Mur - ray, just one step I'll be
(8)
B
C#m7
Bdim/D
B/D#
E7
free! One small step, just so you should - n't
f
mf
(8)

Gdim/E G7/E F♯ Em/F♯ F/F♯ F♯ Em/F♯ F/F♯
wor - ry, I'll be free and you'll be rid of me. Is - n't that
F♯ F♯7♯9 F♯7 B5 N.C.
eas - y, Mur - ray? Watch me... You think this is may-be a
joke? Well it's no joke, Mur-ray!
ad lib.
Spoken: "Murray?"
Sung: It looks like they're form-ing a crowd, like eight y -
B7
repeat ad lib.

E9
Eb9
D9
Db9
five, at the most. Still front page of the Post. Mur, I
C9
F+
think it's Mau-ry Po - vich! And Con - nie, too!
Spoken: "Hi, Connie!"
D6/E
E(add2)
D6/E
Sung: Now you'll fi - n'lly make
mf
E5
D6/E
E(add2)
Bm/E
E7
D6/E
your moth - er proud, since she nev - er liked me an -

E(add2)
D6/E
E5
- y - way. "Look! She's throw - ing dia - monds to the crowd!" You
F♯
G/F♯
A♭/F♯
A/F♯
B♭/F♯
B/F♯
just say the word and I'll come back in - side, but un - til then I'll be hap - py just to
C/F♯
G♯/F♯
E9
know that I can al-ways go and take one step, one ti - ny step. Yes,
mf
8vb
E♭9
D9
E7
B
C♯m7
Bdim/D
B/D♯
Mur - ray, just one step. A - di - os!
f
(8)

E7
E9
Gdim/E
G7/E
One small step. Hon - ey, you bet - ter hur - ry!
mf
(8)
F♯
Em/F♯
F/F♯
F♯
Em/F♯
F/F♯
Oh, yes sir! Bet - ter give up that fur! Take it from
p
p
F♯
F♯7♯9
F♯7
me, ol' Mur - ray, here I...
f
B5
N.C.
Spoken: "Whoops! I almost fell, Murray! The mother
of your children splattered across Park Avenue
in a bloody heap, Murray. And it's all your... fault!"
Sung: Yes, it's
(1st time only)
mp
repeat ad lib.
ff

E9
Eb9/E
E9
Eb9/E
E9
you who made the mon - ey, cause it's you who owns the store. So if you don't want to spend
mf
8vb
Eb9/E
E9
A/E E7 A/E
E9
Eb9/E
it, that's your right. But it's you who bought the pent - house on the
(8)
E9
C#7
F#7
fif - ty - sev-enth floor, so good - night, cheap - skate, good - night.
(8)
loco
B N.C.
You think I don't know a-bout her? Well, I do, Mur ray. You
ff
f

E9
Eb9
think I don't know a - bout that, or the things that _ you say to your
mf
mp
D9
Db9
C9
friends ev - 'ry - day? I'm em - bar - rass - ing. _ I'm fat. I'm de -
mand - ing, I'm con - troll - ing... or what-ev - er.
F+
Per - haps it's true . . .

D6/E
E(add2)
D6/E
E5
Here's the place where I get what I've earned.
mf
D6/E
E(add2)
Bm7/E
E7
D6/E
Why keep cry - ing? Why be mis - 'ra - ble?
E(add2)
D6/E
E5
Look - it, Mu - ray: Some - bod - y's con - cerned!
F#
G/F#
A♭/F#
A/F#
F#
G/F#
A♭/F#
A/F#
Trust in the wind and I'll land on the crowd.
No more com-plain-ing I'm trash - y or loud.
subito mp

F♯ G/F♯ A♭/F♯ A/F♯ D/F♯ B/F♯ F♯7♭5 F♯maj7
What a sen-sa-tion-al fuck-ing ex-per-i-ence! Fi-nal-ly Mur-ray! I'm get-ting at-ten-tion! And
E9 A/E E7
just one step! Look at where one step leads you: One small step
8va
loco
ff
B C♯m7 Bdim/D B/D♯ B C♯m7 Bdim/D B/D♯
takes you high!
8va
ff
E9 A7/E G7/E F♯
Just one step down from the man who needs you! Fuck the
loco
mp

Em/F♯
F/F♯
F♯
fur: Just _ send it back to her! So, _ fare thee well, and Mur - ray,
F♯7♯9
F♯7
B N.C.
watch me fly!
(Vamp till out of breath) Spoken:
"Murray! I'm serious. Murray! Murray?" (GASP!)
Vamp
subito p

THE MAN THAT GOT AWAY

from the Motion Picture *A Star Is Born*

Lyric by IRA GERSHWIN
Music by HAROLD ARLEN

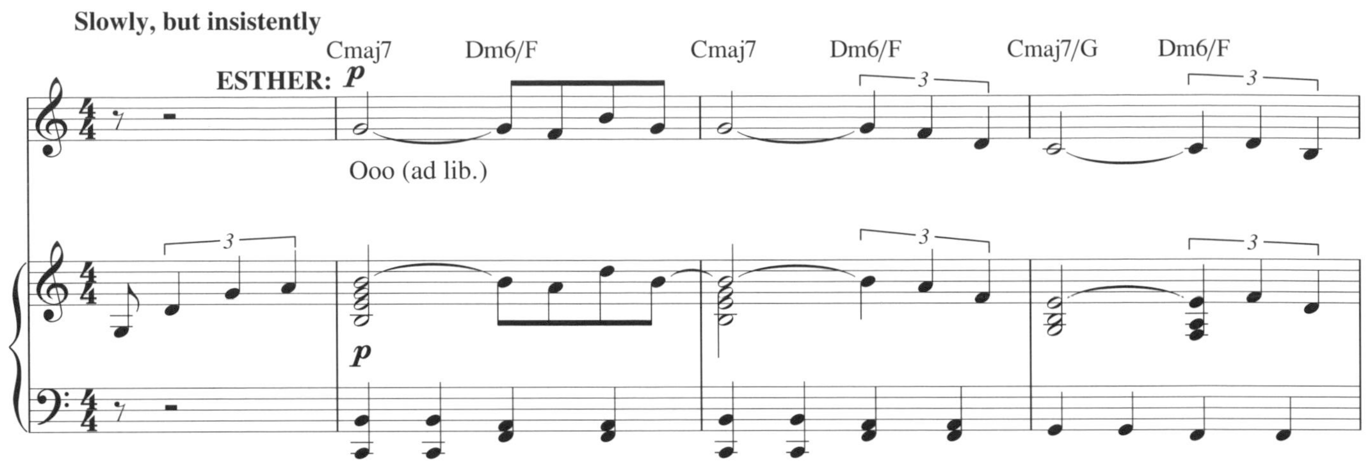

C
A7♯5(♭9)
A7♭9
man that got a - way.
No
Dm11
G7
Edim7
more his ea - ger call;
The writ-ing's on the wall,
A7♭9
Dm11
G7
The dreams you dream'd have all gone a -
C
C7
C6
G7♯9
G9
G7♭9
G7
C6
C7
Cmaj7
C7
stray.
The man that won you has
mf
mp

C6 C7 Cmaj7 C7 Dm7 B♭/D G Gm
run of and un - done you. That great be - gin - ning Has
mp
mp
F9 F♯9 G9 C6 Dm7
seen the fi - nal inn - ing. Don't know what hap - pened, It's
C Dm/G C6 F/C Am/C A7♯5
all a cra - zy game!
No
mf
ff
F6 G9 G+(add9) C6/9
more that all - time thrill,
For you've been through the
f

A7♯5(♭9) A7 Dm7 C6/E Dm9 Fm/G
mill, And nev - er a new love will Be the
mf
C A♭m A(add2) B♭(add2) B(add2) C(add2) A7♭9
same. Good rid - dance! Good- bye!
ff
mf
D9 Bm E♭/D
trick of his you're on
E♭/G Em/G C6 Dm7/C
to; But, fools will be

Cmaj7/G F6 C/E Am/C E♭6 G7♭13 G13
mp
fools, And where's he gone to? The
cresc.
ff
C6 C7 Cmaj7 C7 C6 C7 Cmaj7 C7 Dm7 B♭/D G7 Gm7
road gets rough - er, It's lone - li - er and tough - er, With hope you burn up, To -
mp
F7 F♯7 G7 C Dm7 C6 Dm/G C6 F/C
mor - row he will turn up. There's just no let - up The live - long night and
D6/E A7♯5
day! E - ver

F6
F♯dim
C6/G
since this world be - gan
There is noth - ing sad - der than
ff
A7♯5
A7
A9
Freely
Dm7
Em7
Fmaj7
G7♭9
mf
A one man wo - man look - ing for the man that got a -
mp
rit.
Cmaj7
C7
C
Cmaj7
C7
G7♯9
a tempo
mp
way.
The man that got a -
a tempo
p
rit.
Cmaj7
Dm6/F
Cmaj7
Dm6/F
Cmaj7
way.
rit.
pp

GIMME GIMME

from *Thoroughly Modern Millie*

Music by JEANINE TESORI
Lyrics by DICK SCANLAN

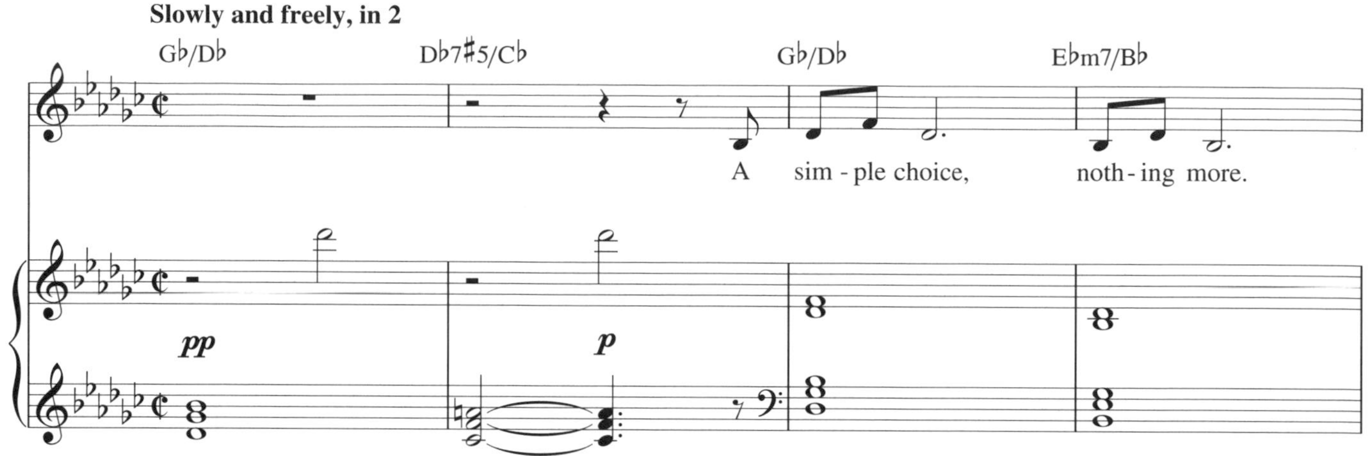

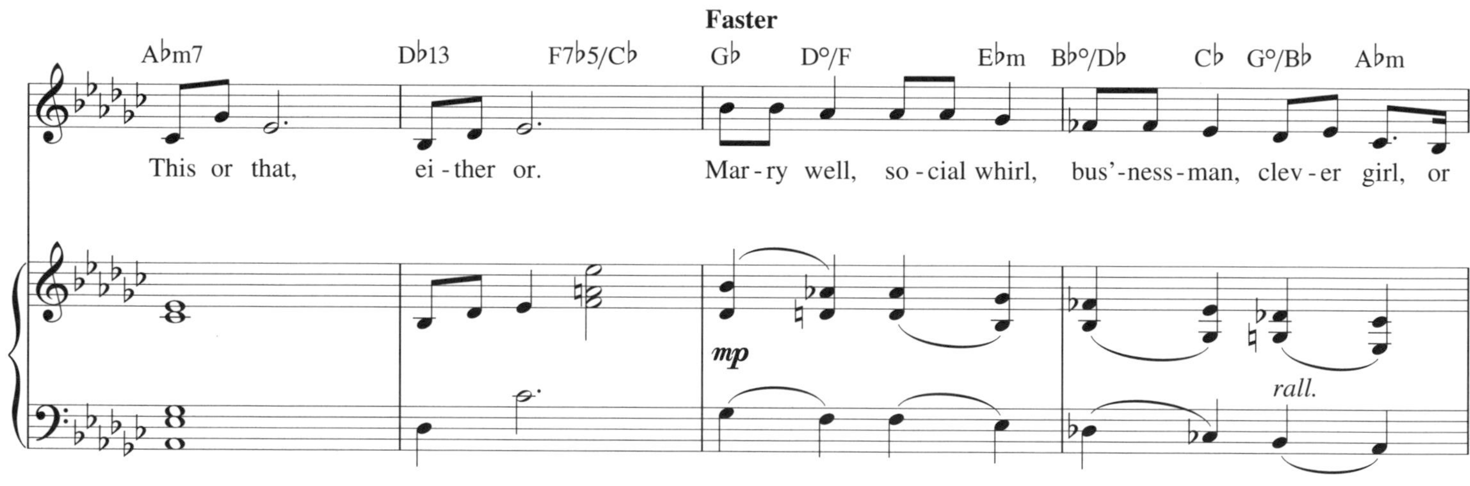

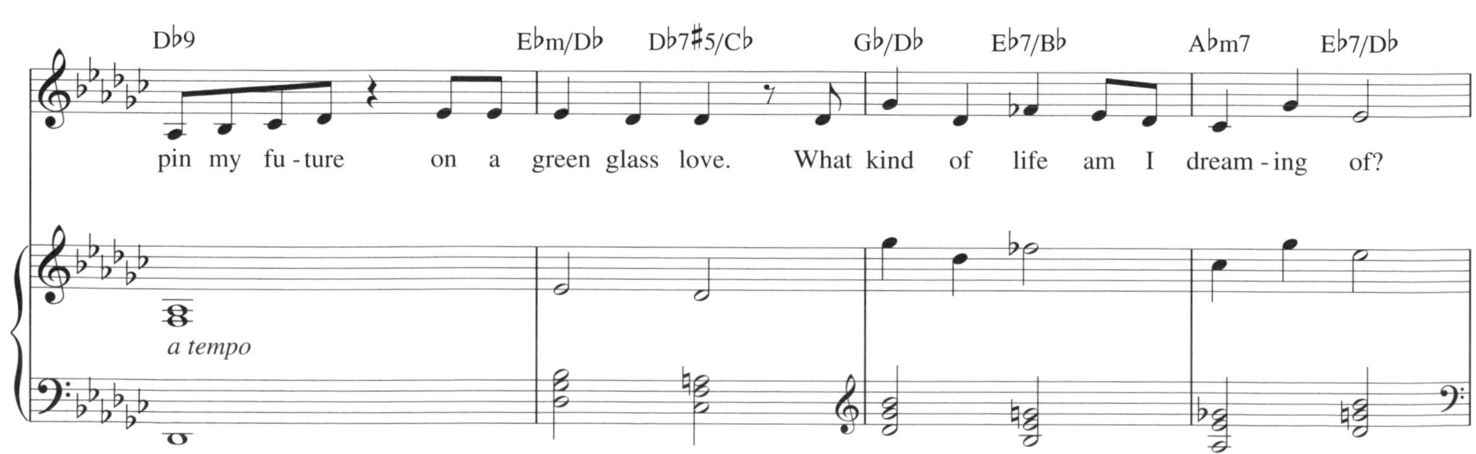

Moderately slow (♫ = ♩♪) (not a wide swing)
N.C.
E6/B
B+add2
E6/B
I say:
Gim-me gim-me...
Gim-me gim-me...
B+add2
E6/B
B+add2
E6/B
Gim-me gim-me
that thing called
love.
B+add2
E6/B
B+add2
E
E/D♯
I want it.
Gim-me gim-me
that thing called
love.
C♯9
C♯9/E♯
F♯7
C7
E/B
I need it.
Highs and lows,
tears and laugh-ter.
Gim-me
hap-py

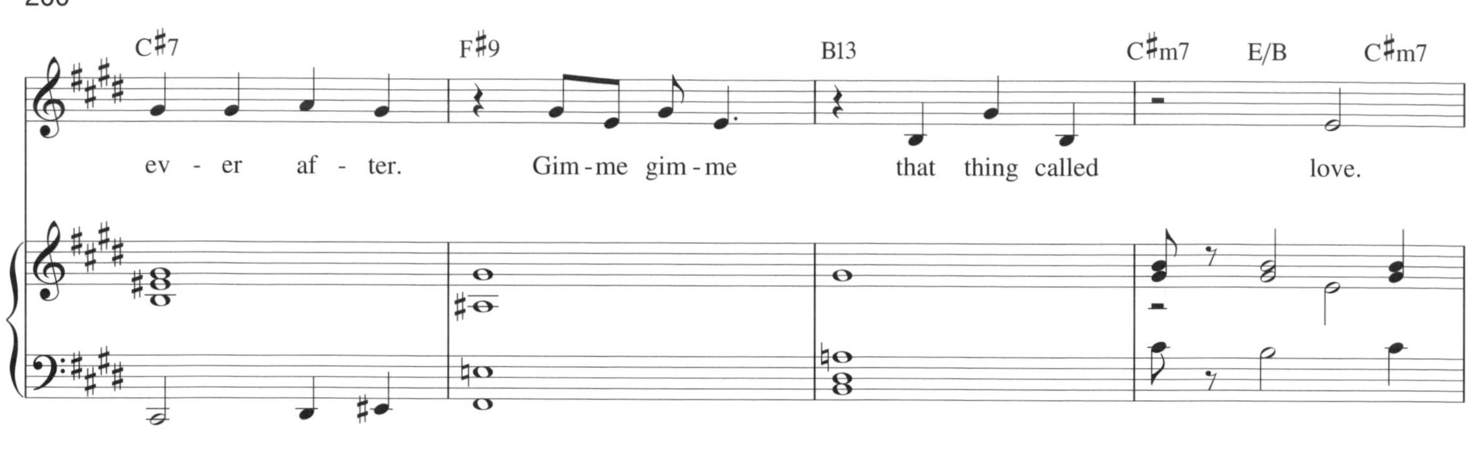
C♯7
F♯9
B13
C♯m7
E/B
C♯m7
ev - er af - ter. Gim-me gim-me that thing called love.

Moderately, with more confidence
B+
B+/C♯
B+
E
B+add2
E
Gim-me gim-me that thing called love.

B+add2
E
B+add2
E
E/D
I crave it. Gim-me gim-me that thing called love.
grad. accel.

C♯7
F♯9
C7
E/B
I'll brave _ it. Thick 'n' thin, rich or poor time. Gim-me years and

C♯7
F♯9
B9
E
C+
C♯m/B
I'll want more time. Gim-me gim-me that thing called love.
cresc.
E
C+
C♯m/B
Spirited, in 2
G6
D+add2
G6
Gim-me gim-me that thing called love.
mf
D+add2
G6
D+add2
G
G/F
I'm free now. Gim-me gim-me that thing called love.
E7♯5
A9
E♭7
G/D
I see now. Fly, dove! Sing, spar-row! Gim-me Cu-pid's

E7
A7
D9
G6
fa - mous ar - row. Gim-me gim-me that thing called love.
Faster
G♯7
G7
G♯7
C♯m
I don't care if he's a no -
cresc.
f
B♭7
A7
B♭7
E♭m
bod - y. In my heart he'll be a some -
B/D♯
D7
bod - y, some - bod - y to love

F6/C
C+add2
F6/C
me.
ff
C9♯5
F6/C
C9♯5
F
F/E♭
I need it.
Gim-me
that thing called
love.
molto rit.
Freely
Moderately and broadly, in 4 (Bring it home!)
D7♯5
N.C.
G7
D♭7
F/C
I wan-nit!
Here I am,
Saint
Val-en-tine!
My
bags are packed;
Faster
D7
B♭6
D♭7/C♭
F/C
I'm first in line.
Aph-ro-di-te,
don't for-get me.
Ro-me-o and
accel.
mf
8vb

D7
B♭6
B♭m6
F/C
N.C.
Ju - li - et me! Fly, dove! Sing, spar-row! Gim - me fat boy's
cresc.
f
D7
G9
C9
fa - mous ar - row! Gim - me gim - me that thing
F6
F6/E♭
Dm7♭5
D♭7
C9
F6
F6/E♭
called love!
ff
Dm7♭5
D♭7
C9
F6
F6/E♭
Dm7♭5
D♭7
C9
E/C
F

POPULAR
from *Wicked*

Music and Lyrics by
STEPHEN SCHWARTZ

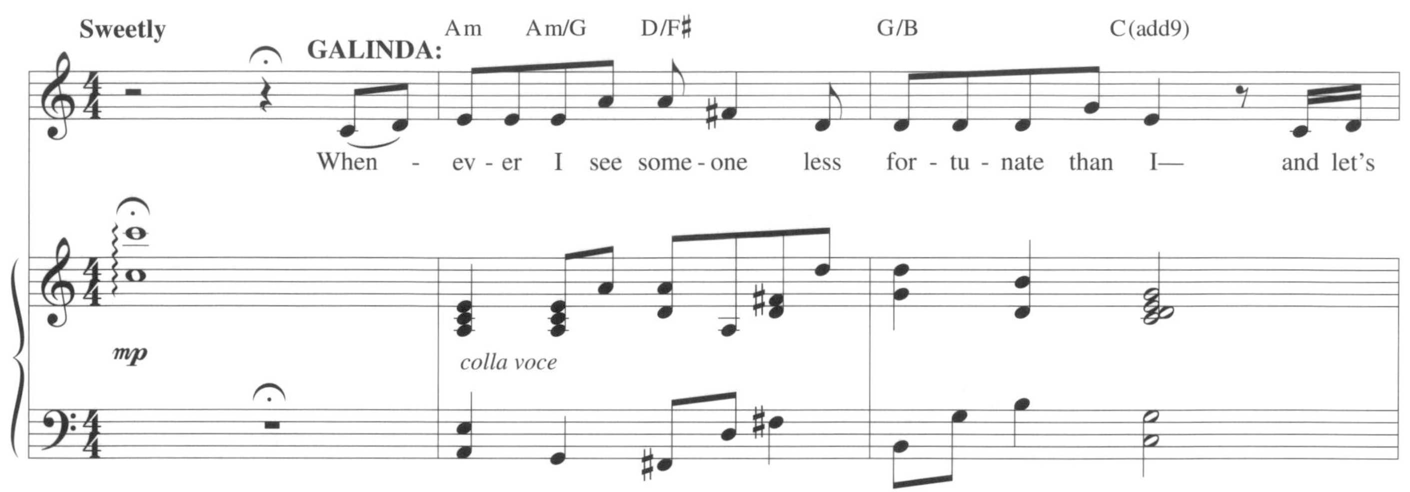

A♭(add9)
B♭(add9)/A♭
Gsus(add9)
G
Gm
C
know I know ex - act - ly what they need! And e - ven in your case, tho' it's the
colla voce
Am7
D/F♯
Gm
B♭/E♭
C(add9)
C
F/B♭
tough - est case I've yet to face, don't wor - ry, I'm de - ter - mined to suc - ceed Fol - low my
C(add9)
G9sus
G9
C
N.C.
ten.
lead and yes, in - deed you will be...
rit.
colla voce
ten.
Bright and bubbly
F
C
B♭sus2
F
C/E
Pop - u - lar, You're gon - na be pop - u - lar! I'll teach you the
p

Dm Am/C Dm Am/C B♭maj7 C
prop - er ploys when you talk to boys, lit - tle ways to flirt and flounce
F A7/E Dm F+/C♯ F/C Bm7♭5 B♭ Gm7
I'll show you what shoes to wear, how to fix your hair, ev - 'ry - thing that
C F C B♭(add9) F
real - ly counts to be pop - u - lar! I'll help you be pop - u - lar!
mf
C/E Dm Am/C Dm Am/C
You'll hang with the right co - horts, you'll be good at sports, know the

B♭maj7
C
A7sus
D
Gm7
slang you've got to know
So let's start, 'cause you've got an
Gm7/B♭
Csus
C
F
Gm7(no5th)
G♯dim7
F/A
aw - f'lly long way to go!
cresc.
D♭
D♭(♭5)/A♭
D♭
D♭(♭5)/A♭
A♭maj7
N.C.
Don't be of - fend - ed by my frank an - al - y - sis
Think of it as per - son - al - i -
sub. mf chugging along
A♭6/9/E♭
D♭m7
D♭m6/A♭
D♭m7
D♭m6/A♭
ty di - al - y - sis
Now that I've cho - sen to be - come a pal, a sis -

E♭
B♭m6/D♭
C
- ter and ad - vis - er there's no - bod - y wis - er, not when it comes to
f
F
C
B♭(add9)
F
C/E
pop - u - lar I know a - bout pop - u - lar! And with an as -
8va
Dm
Am/C
Dm
Am/C
B♭maj7
A7sus
A7/E
sist from me to be who you'll be, in - stead of drear - y who - you - were...
(8va)
Dm
F7/C
B♭
Dm/A
Gm7
C
are... There's noth - ing that can stop you from be - com - ing pop - u -
(8va)
loco
3

F N.C.
F C
ler... lar... La la
R.H.
mf
B♭(add9) F Gm7 B♭ B♭(add9)/C C
la la We're gon - na make you pop - u -
F Gm7(no5th) G♯dim7 F/A A Bm7(no5th) Adim/C A/C♯
lar! When I see de-press - ing crea - tures
f
Dm A/E Dm/F G Am7(no5th) Gdim/B♭ G/B
with un - pre - pos-sess - ing fea - tures, I re - mind them on their own be -

C
A
Bm7(no5th)
Adim/C
A/C♯
half to think of cel - e - brat - ed heads of state— or
straight 8ths
Dm
A/E
Dm/F
G
Am7(no5th)
'spe - cially great— com - mu - ni - ca - tors... Did they have
Gdim/B♭
G/B
C
brains or knowl - edge? Don't make me laugh! They were
F
C
B♭(add9)
F
C/E
pop - u - lar— Please! It's all— a - bout pop - u - lar! It's not— a - bout

Dm Am/C Dm Am/C B♭maj7 A7sus A7 Dm7 G9
ap - ti - tude, it's the way you're viewed, so it's ver - y shrewd to be
Gm7 B♭ Csus C F
ver - y, ver - y pop - u - lar like me! And tho'
poco rall.
Freely
Dm Am/C Dm Am/C B♭maj7 E7sus A7/G
you pro - test your dis - in - ter - est, I know clan - des - tine - ly
mp colla voce
A tempo
Dm G Gm7 B♭ Csus C
You're gon - na grin and bear it your new-found pop - u - lar - it -
f

F
N.C.
F
C
y
La
la
8va
R.H.
Bb(add9)
F
Gm7
Bb
la
la
You'll
be
pop - u - lar
Just
not
(8va)
loco
Gm7
Bb
Csus
C
quite
as
pop - u - lar
as
3
F
C
Bb(add9)
C
F
me!

I'M NOT THAT GIRL

from *Wicked*

Music and Lyrics by
STEPHEN SCHWARTZ

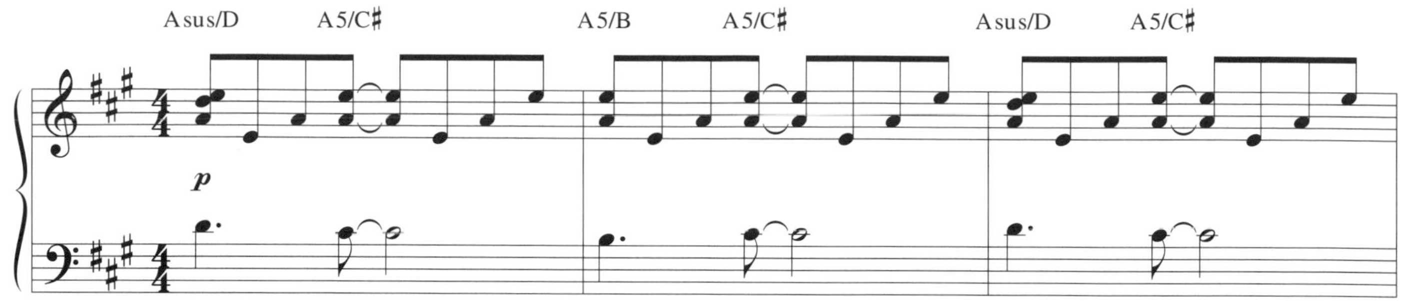

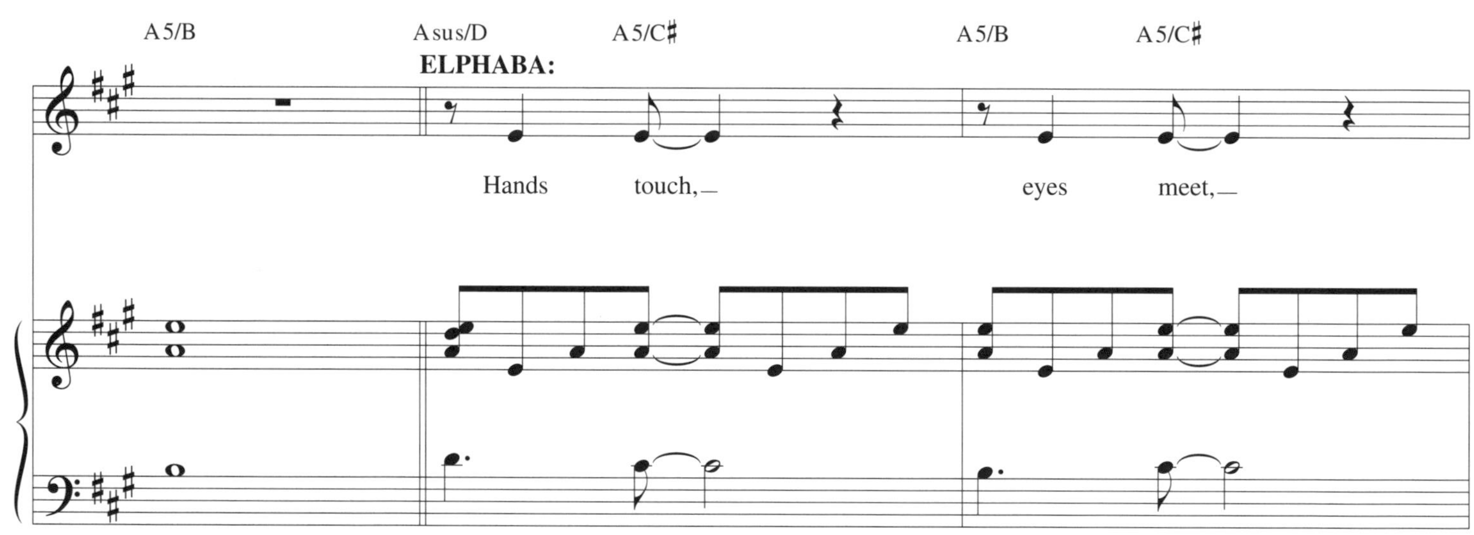

D(add9) D E/G♯ C♯m7 A/C♯ Bm A/D
whirl, He could be that boy, but I'm not that
Esus E Asus/D A5/C♯ A5/B A5/C♯
girl. Don't dream too far,
mp
Asus/D A5/C♯ E/B A D/F♯ F♯m E/G♯
Don't lose sight of who you are. Don't re-mem - ber that rush of
C♯m7 A/C♯ Bm7 A/D
joy. He could be that boy, I'm not that girl.

1:15 lyric
1:00
A
F
B♭/D
E♭
Ev - 'ry so of - ten we long to steal to the
mf
A♭maj7/C
D♭(add9)
Em
A/C♯
land of What-Might - Have - Been, But that does - n't soft - en the
F♯7/A♯
Bm
C
Bsus
Asus/B♭
E7/B♭
ache we feel when re - al - i - ty sets back in.
poco rit.
Tempo I
Asus/D
A5/D
A5/B
A5/C♯
Asus/D
A5/C♯
Blithe smile, lithe limb, She who's win - some,

E/B
A
D/F♯
F♯m
E/G♯
D(add9)
E(add2)/G♯
she wins him.
Gold hair
with a gen-tle
curl
That's the girl he
C♯m7
A/C♯
Bm7
A/D
Esus
chose,
and heav - en
knows,
E
Asus/D
A5/C♯
A5/B
A5/C♯
I'm not
that
girl.
p
Asus/D
A5/C♯
Asus/B
Asus/D
A5/C♯
Don't
wish,
pp

A5/B
A5/C♯
Asus/D
A5/C♯
E/B
A
don't start.
Wish-ing on-ly wounds the heart.
cresc.
A Tempo
D/F♯
F♯m
E/G♯
D(add9)
D
E/G♯
I was-n't born for the rose and pearl,
There's a girl I
mf
rit.
warmly
C♯m7
A/C♯
Bm7
A/D
Esus
know—
He loves her so,
poco rit.
E
Asus/D
A5/C♯
E/B
I'm not that girl…
opt.
a tempo
p
rit.

THE WIZARD AND I

from *Wicked*

Music and Lyrics by
STEPHEN SCHWARTZ

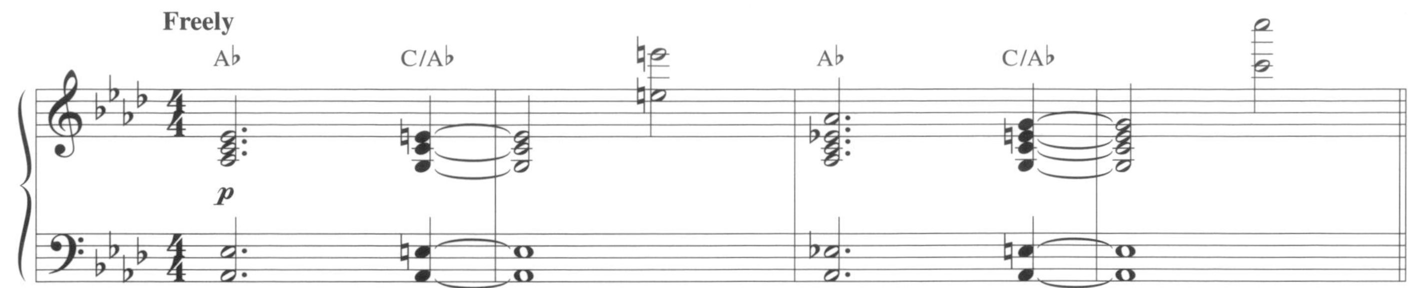

B♭m7 E♭7/G Cm7 G♭(add9)
if I make good! So I'll make
gliss.
rit.

Pulsing with excitement

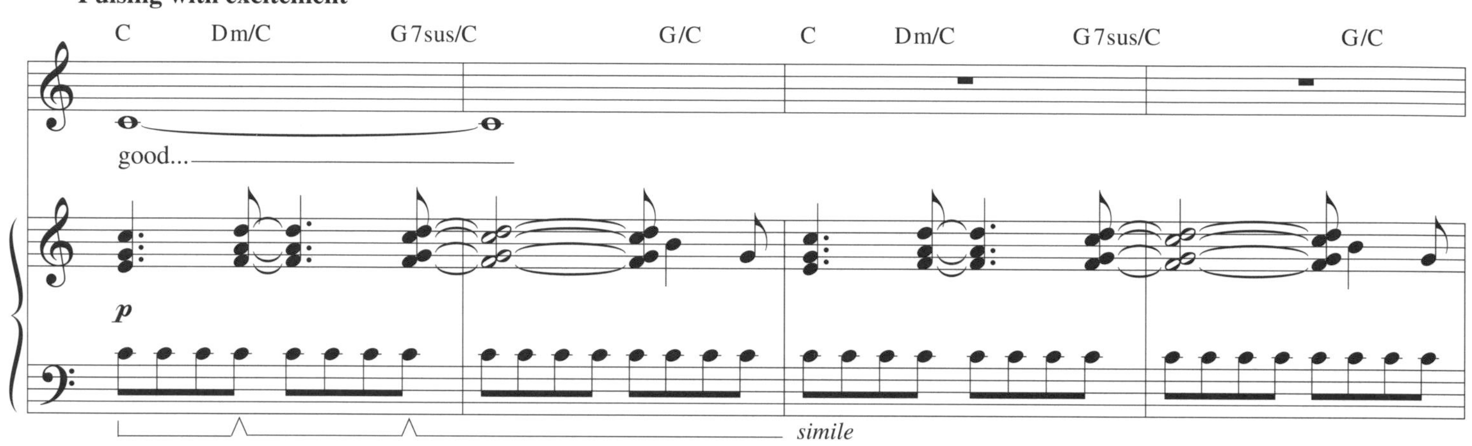
C Dm/C G7sus/C G/C C Dm/C G7sus/C G/C
good...
p
simile

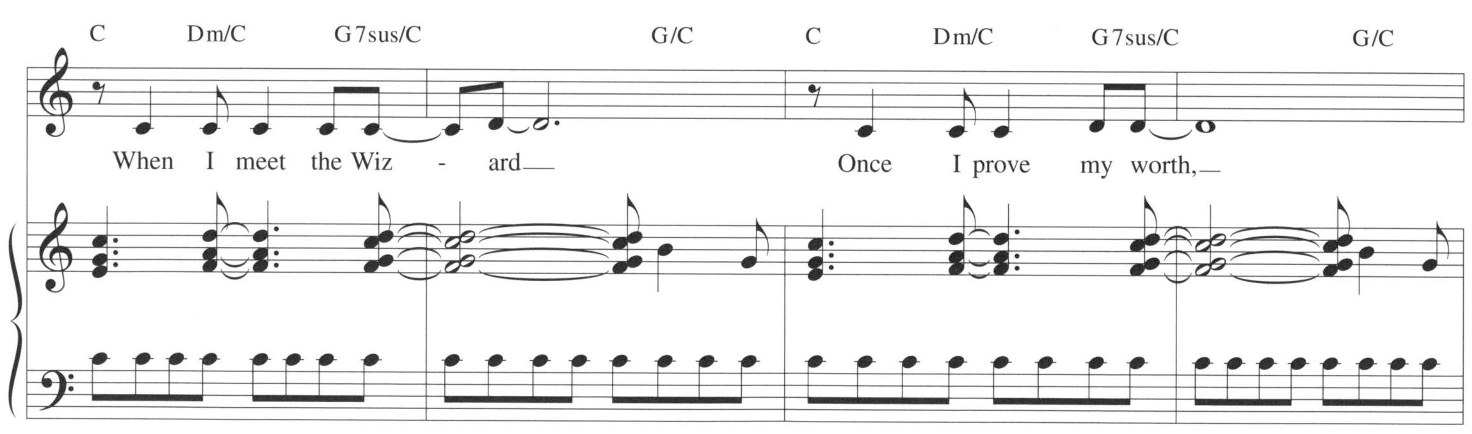
C Dm/C G7sus/C G/C C Dm/C G7sus/C G/C
When I meet the Wiz - ard Once I prove my worth,

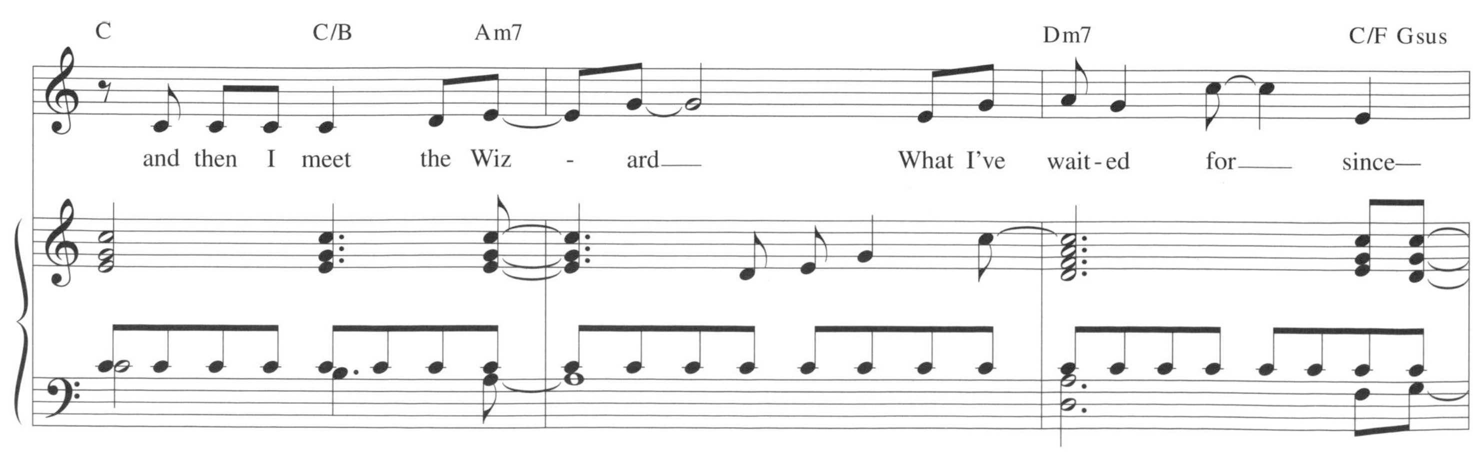
C C/B Am7 Dm7 C/F Gsus
and then I meet the Wiz - ard What I've wait-ed for since

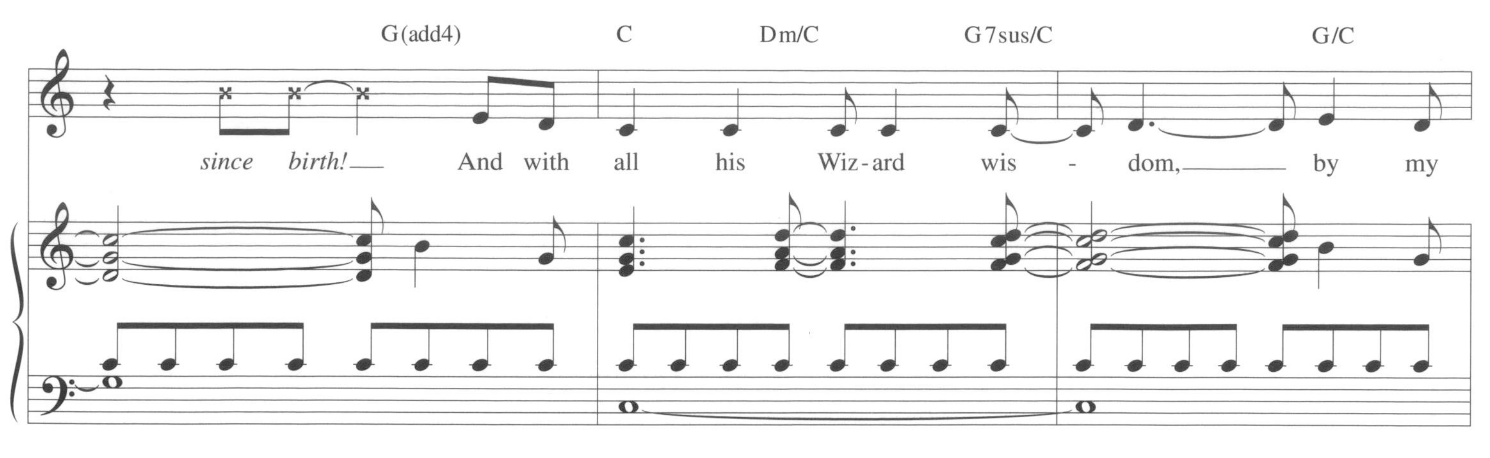
G(add4)
C
Dm/C
G7sus/C
G/C
since birth! And with all his Wiz-ard wis - dom, by my

C
Em
B♭maj7/F
looks, he won't be blind - ed… Do you think the Wiz - ard is

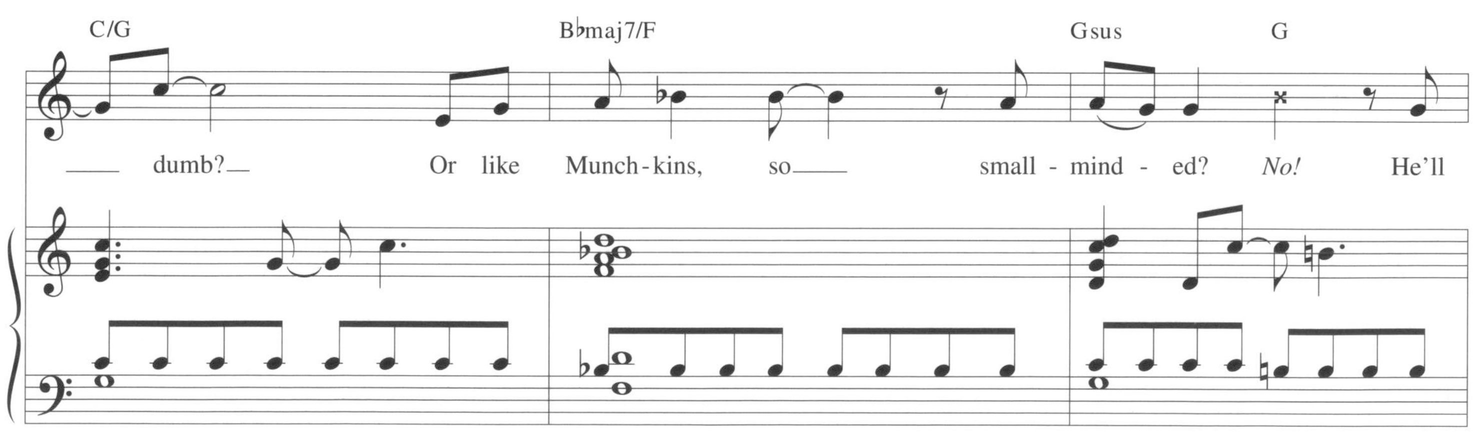
C/G
B♭maj7/F
Gsus
G
dumb? Or like Munch-kins, so small - mind - ed? No! He'll

Am7
Dm7(add4)
G/B
C/E
Am7
Dm7(add4)
say to me: "I see who you tru - ly are: A girl on whom I can re -

Gsus G C Dm7 C/E Fsus F
ly!" And that's how we'll be - gin, the Wiz - ard and I...
C Dm7 Gsus C Dm7 Gsus
mf
C Dm7 Gsus G C Dm7 Gsus
Once I'm with the Wiz - ard, my whole life will change.
bring out
C C/B Am7
'Cause once you're with the Wiz - ard,

Dm7 C/F Gsus C Dm7 Gm7(add4)
no one thinks you're strange. No fa - ther is not proud of
simile
C C/B Em7
you; no sis - ter acts a - shamed. And
F/B♭ Csus2 F/C C F/B♭ B♭maj7 Gsus
all of Oz has to love you, when by the Wiz - ard, you're ac - claimed.
G Am7 Dm7 G/B C/E
And this gift or this curse I have in - side,

Am7
Dm7
Gsus
G
C
Dm7
C/E
May - be at last I'll know why, as we work hand in hand,
Più mosso
Fsus
F
Amaj7
the Wiz - ard and I!
And
ad lib.
Dmaj9
C♯m11
Dmaj9
one day, he'll say to me: "El - pha - ba, a girl who is so su -
mf
C♯m11
Fmaj9
Em7(add4)
pe - ri - or—
Should - n't a girl who's so good in - side

Dm7(add4)
Em7(add4)
Cm9
B♭/E♭
F(add4)
have a match - ing ex - te - ri - or? And since folks here to an ab -
rhythmically
B♭(add9)/D
Cm9
B♭/E♭
F(add4)
B♭(add9)/D
surd de - gree seem fix - at - ed on your ver - di - gris, Would
Freely
D♭
Csus
C
B♭m7
it be all right by you, if I de - green - i - fy
dim. e rall.
mp
A tempo
Csus
C
Am7
Dm7
G/B
C/E
you?" And though of course that's not im - por - tant to me,

Am7
Dm7
Gsus
G
C
Csus/D
C/E
"All right, why not?" I'll re - ply. Oh, what a pair we'll be
mf
Fsus F
Am
Dm7
Gsus
G
C
Dm7
C/E
The Wiz-ard and I!
What a pair we'll be,
Dreamily
Fsus
F
C♭maj9♯11
The Wiz - ard and...
f
subito p
With pedal
E♭m9
C♭maj9♯11
G♭maj9/D♭
Un - lim - it - ed
My fu-ture is
un - lim - it -

G♭maj7
C♭maj9♯11
B♭m11
ed… And I've just had a vi - sion al - most like a proph - e -
Freely
E♭m11
A♭dim/E♭♭
G♭/D♭
D♭9sus
G♭/D♭
D♭9sus
cy— I know, it sounds tru - ly cra - zy, and true, the vi - sion's ha - zy,
rit.
A(add9)
Amaj7
A6
Dmaj9
G♭/D♭
F/D♭
but I swear, some - day there'll be a cel - e - bra - tion through - out Oz that's
mf warmly
A tempo
C♭/D♭
B♭7sus
B♭7
B♭7sus
B♭7
all to do with me!
rall.
f

Broadly
Gm7
Gm9
B♭maj7/C
C7
B
Bsus/C♯
And I'll stand there with the Wiz - ard, feel - ing things I've nev - er felt,
cresc.
rall.
gliss.
ff
Bsus/F♯
accel.
Bsus2/A♯
G♯m7
Bsus/G♯
C♯m7
B/E
F♯sus
And though I'd nev - er show it, I'll be so hap - py, I could melt!
poco a poco accel.
Bright, triumphant
F♯
F♯/A♯
B/D♯
And so it will be for the rest of my life, and I'll

G♯m7 Bsus/C♯ F♯5 F♯sus F♯ B C♯m7 B/D♯ Esus
want noth - ing else till I die! Held in such high es - teem,
subito mf
E C Dm7 C/E Fsus F
when peo - ple see me, they will scream for half of
cresc.
C Csus/D C/E Fm(maj7)/A♭ G7sus
Oz - 's fav - 'rite team: The Wiz - ard and
f
molto rall.
A tempo
C Dm7 G Am(add9) Am Fmaj9 D♭(add♯4) B(add♭6) C
I!
ff
rall.

LOOK AT ME NOW
from *The Wild Party*

Words and Music by
ANDREW LIPPA

N.C.
E7+
I was born
A6
C#9#5
C#7#5
F#m7
in a ditch in West Vir - gin -
A/E
D#m7♭5
Dm9
- ia. Ran a - way from home at ten.
C#m7♭5
F#m7♭5
Bm11
Crawled right out of that ditch

C♯m/E
C/D
C♯7♯9
F♯7♯5(♭9)
and
ho - ly
cow!
Bm7
(E)
(E/F)
(E/G)
Just take a look at me now.
E+/G♯
A
C♯13
G9
I've been learn - ing a trade,
I've
F♯m
N.C.
D♯m7♭5
Dm6
slung the hash
for
more
than just
Even 8th's
Swing

C#m7♭5
F#7#9
a cou - ple men.
I've been
8va
mp
Bm11
Bm7/F#
C#m/E
C/D
C#7#9
pil - lowed and paid for wah wah wow!
mf
F#7#9
Bm7
F#m/C#
D6
Dmaj7/E
But won't you look at me now!
(A)

D6
F/G
G13
A/E
Emaj7#5
Look at me now taking a bow. I've been to Hell and back.
(N.C.)
D6
Look at me now,
F/G
F6
A/E
F#m7
C
E7#5(♭9)
hap-py and how, I met a swell named Mis-ter Black.
Am13/E
N.C.
Spoken: Give me a bottle of bourbon and half a chicken and I'll conquer the world!

E7+
A6
C#9#5
I got life in me yet and
F#m7
A/E
D#m7♭5
let me tell you the South is gon - na
Dm9
G9
N.C.
Fmaj7/E
rise a - gain. When you
Bm7
C#m/E
C/D
C#7#9
F#6(♭9)
start in a ditch you quick - ly learn to plow!

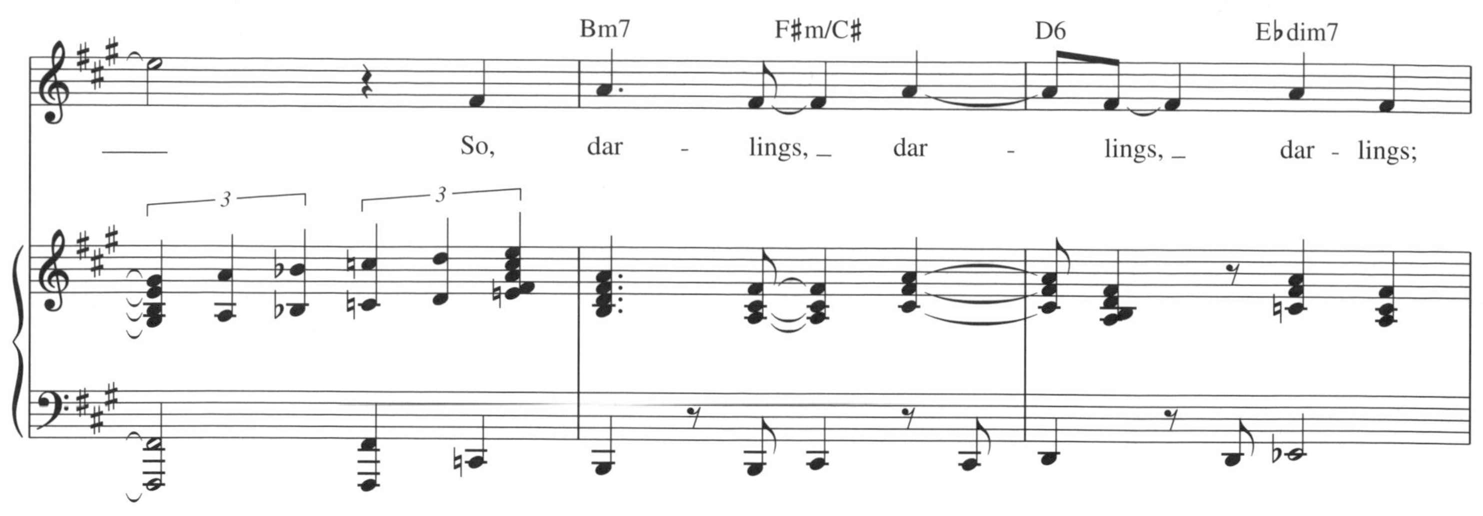
Bm7
F♯m/C♯
D6
E♭dim7
So, dar - lings, dar - lings, dar - lings;

C/E
E7+
D♯m7♭5
take a damn good look, look at me now!

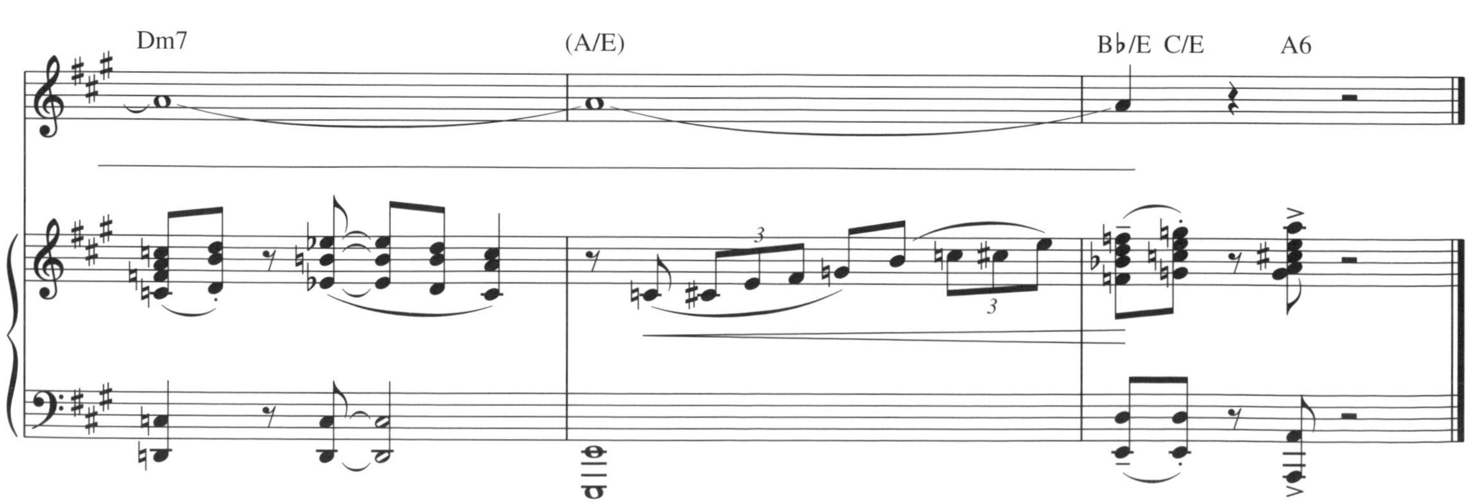
Dm7
(A/E)
B♭/E C/E
A6

HOW DID WE COME TO THIS?

from *The Wild Party*

Words and Music by
ANDREW LIPPA

F♯m7♭5
G♯m7
C♯13♯9
neigh - bor,
smil - ing through a
hiss.
F♯m9
Aadd9/B
Amadd9/B
G♯7♭5
C♯m7
How
did
we
come
to
this?
F♯m7
B7sus
B(♭9♭5)
E
E+
We're all
a - mused,
rit.
a tempo
keep it moving
8vb
E
Emaj7♯5
C♯m/E
E+
we're all
in - spired.
So
cun - ning,
so
clev - er,
(8vb)

E
D/E
E9
Aadd9
and so ad - mired.
Eas - y to be
mf
(8vb)
F#m7b5
G#m9
C#7#9
an - gry,
eas - y to dis - miss.
(8vb)
F#m9
B7sus
E
How did we come to this?
mp
mf
(8vb)
D#m7b5
G#m7b9
G#m7/C#
C#m7
G#m7/C#
C#m7
D#m7b5
G#m7b9
G#m7#9
May - be I've been liv - ing in a day - dream.
May - be I've been talk - ing in my
f
8vb
8vb

C#maj7
F#m7
F#m7/B
Emaj7
Amaj7
sleep.
If I've been a - wake,
par - don my mis - take,
8vb
8vb
D#m7♭5
C7♭5
B6/9
D7sus/B
E
rit.
but time is run - ning low and
talk is grow - ing cheap.
We play our
rit.
8vb
E+
E
G#/E
C#m/E
games.
We place out
bets.
No wit - ness,
(8vb)
E+
E
D6/E
E9
Aadd9
no weak - ness,
and no re - grets.
Fill - ing up with
(8vb)

F#m7♭5
G#m9
C#+(#9) C#7+(♭9) F#m7(add11)
F#m9
fren - zy.
Kill-ing with a
kiss.
How did we
(8vb)
8vb
B
B7
B7#5/A
G#m7♭5
Bm/C#
C#7
Slower
F#9
D9#11
all
come to
this?
Time goes by,
plans grow stale,
rit.
ff
8vb
8vb
Very slow
G#m9
C#7♭9
F#m9
B7sus
peo - ple die and par - ties fail.
How did we come to
rit.
p
colla voce
E
D9
E6
this?
move along
mf
poco rit.
mp
8vb

ONE HUNDRED EASY WAYS TO LOSE A MAN

from *Wonderful Town*

Lyrics by BETTY COMDEN
and ADOLPH GREEN
Music by LEONARD BERNSTEIN

(Spoken flatly)
Just leap out, crawl under the car, say it's the gasket, and fix it in two seconds flat with a bobby pin.
rall.
bat your eyes and say, "What a ro - man - tic spot we're in."
rall.
a tempo
That's a good way to lose a man.
He takes you to a base - ball game, you
f
a tempo
fz
p
sit knee to knee.
He says, "The next man up at bat will bunt, you'll see."
Don't
Just say, "Bunt? Are you nuts?! With no outs, two men on base, and a left-handed batter coming up, he'll walk right into a triple play, just like it happened in the fifth game of the World Series in 1923."
rall.
say, "Oooh, what's a bunt? This game's too hard for lit - tle me."
rall.

a tempo
Faster (but light)
That's a sure way to lose a man. A sure, sure, sure, sure
way to lose a man, A splen-did way to lose a man. Just throw your
Tempo I
know-ledge in his face, He'll nev-er try for sec-ond base.
(spoken)
(sung)
Nine-ty-eight ways to go. The third way to lose a man: The

life - guard at the beach that all the girl - ies a dore
Swims
rall.
brave - ly out to save you through the o - cean's roar,
Don't say, "Oh, thanks, I would have drowned in
rall.
Just push his head under water and yell, "Last one in is a rotten egg" and race him back to shore.
a tempo
just one sec - ond more."
That's a swell way to lose a man.
You've
a tempo
fz
p
f
found your per - fect mate and it's been love from the start.
He

rall.
whis - pers, "You're the one to who I give my heart." Don't say, "I love you, too, my dear, let's
rall.
Just say, "I'm afraid you've made a grammatical error. It's not "To who I give my heart," it's "To whom I give my heart." -- You see, with the use of the preposition "to," "who" becomes the indirect object, making the use of "whom" imperative; which I can easily show you by drawing a simple chart."
a tempo
nev - er, nev - er part." That's a fine way to lose a man. A
f a tempo
p
Tempo II (Faster)
fine, fine, fine, fine way to lose a man, A dan - dy way to lose a
Slow and free
man. Just be more well in - formed than he, You'll nev - er

hear "Oh, prom - ise me." Just show him where his gram - mar errs, Then mark your
with a beat
f
Tempo I
tow - els "Hers" and "Hers." Yes, girls, you too can lose your man, if you will
use Ruth Sher-wood's plan: "One Hun - dred Eas - y Ways To
Lose A Man!"

SHOPPING AROUND
from *Wish You Were Here*

Words and Music by
HAROLD ROME

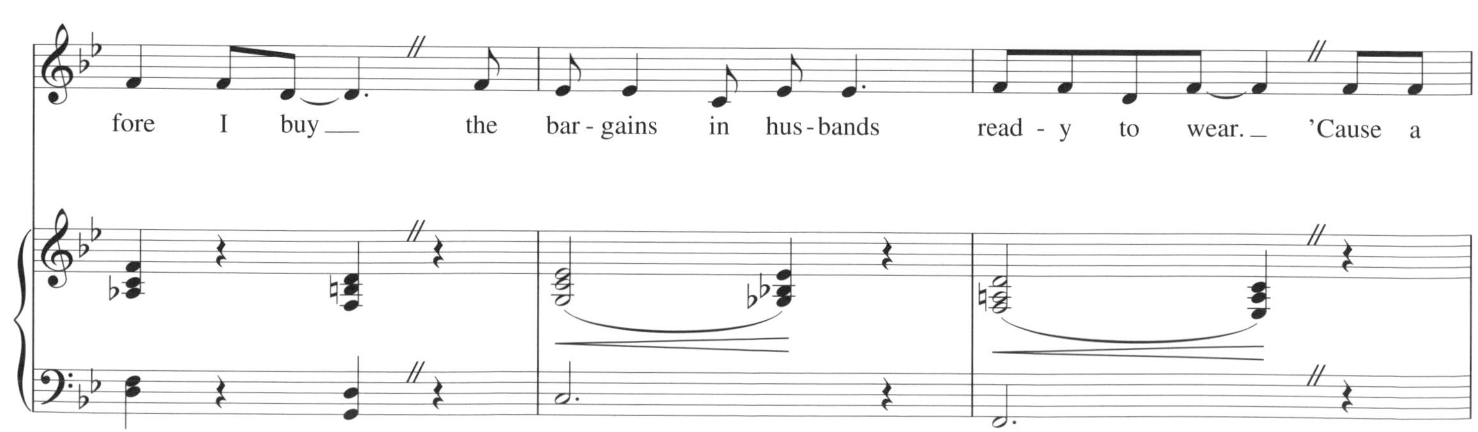

man is-n't like an ex-pen-sive sweat-er or de-part-ment store dress on the
pp
rack. If you wrap him up and take him home and then see some-thing bet-ter,
pp
Moderato (in 4) Swing
No-bod-y, but no-bod-y will take him back!
mf
Refrain (smoothly and not fast)
So, I'm shop-ping a-round, just
p

look - in'.
Where men are con - cerned,
I'm just shop - pin' a - round.
A
girl must com - pare men for wear and for tear be - fore she buys.
If she wants the best, then she just has to test
cresc.
f

f
All kinds of mer - chan - dise!
So while I'm still young,
p
I'm test - ing.
Don't
want to get stung,
No sir, not lit - tle me.
The bride groom to be car ries no guar an tee,
So if
pp
cresc.

You want the best to be found, You've got - ta keep shop - pin',
lei - sure - ly shop - pin',
Not buy - in',
just shop - pin' a - round! You
mp
pp
ff

don't buy the first pair of shoes from the clerk. You don't buy per - fume till you
pp
spray it. You don't buy a clock till you're sure it will work. You
don't buy a pia - no till you play it. A new vac - uum clean - er may
p
sf
be a sen - sa - tion, But la - dies al - ways get a free trial
f

dem - on - stra - tion!
sf
sf
f
p
You've got to be - ware, sam - ple things here and there, know
p
what they do.
You've got to be sure that the
goods will en - dure,
Last you a life - time through!
So
sfz

while there's a chance, I'm sampling.
I'm taking romance In the smorgasbord
way. From the last organ note, love is
all table d'hote, So you must choose the best to be found. That's why I keep
p
leggiero
cresc.
f

shop - pin',
Lei - sure - ly
shop - pin',
f
Not
buy - in',
Just
shop - pin'
a - round.
sffz